Family Circle | **buffet entertaining cookbook**

Family Circle®

BUFFET ENTERTAINING COOKBOOK

FAMILY CIRCLE LIBRARY OF CREATIVE COOKING

A Practical Guide to creative cooking containing special material from Family Circle
Magazine and the Family Circle Illustrated Library of Cooking

ROCKVILLE HOUSE PUBLISHERS
GARDEN CITY, NEW YORK 11530

on the cover:
A selection of buffet standouts: (clockwise, from bottom), **Chicken and Chinese Cabbage Salad, Apricot Wheat Germ Bread, Marinated Chick Peas and Tuna and Artichoke Salad,** and **Orange-Whole Wheat Bread.**

on the back cover:
Sliced pineapples and preserved ginger top this **Baked Lemon-Ginger Ham** (bottom), and a goose is the star attraction at a **Christmas Buffet** (top).

opposite title page:
A roast beef platter with buttery rolls, a warming tray filled with cooked vegetables, and a rich molded dessert will guarantee the success of any buffet party.

Publishing Staff

Editor: MALCOLM E. ROBINSON
Design and Layout: MARGOT L. WOLF
Production Editor: DONALD D. WOLF

For Family Circle

Editorial Director: ARTHUR M. HETTICH
Editor Family Circle Books: MARIE T. WALSH
Assistant Editor: CERI E. HADDA

A QUICK METRIC TABLE FOR COOKS

Liquid Measures

1 liter	4¼ cups (1 quart + ¼ cup or 34 fluid ounces)	1 gallon	3.785 liters
1 demiliter (½ liter)	2⅛ cups (1 pint + ⅛ cups or 17 fluid ounces)	1 quart	0.946 liter
1 deciliter (1/10 liter)	A scant ½ cup or 3.4 fluid ounces	1 pint	0.473 liter
1 centiliter (1/100 liter)	Approximately 2 teaspoons or .34 fluid ounce	1 cup	0.237 liter or 237 milliliters
1 milliliter (1/1000 liter)	Approximately 1/5 teaspoon or .034 fluid ounce	1 tbsp.	Approximately 1.5 centiliters or 15 milliliters

Weights

1 kilogram	2.205 pounds	1 pound	0.454 kilogram or 453.6 grams
500 grams	1.103 pounds or about 17.5 ounces	½ pound	0.226 kilogram or 226.8 grams
100 grams	3.5 ounces	¼ pound	0.113 kilogram or 113.4 grams
10 grams	.35 ounce	1 ounce	28.35 grams
1 gram	0.035 ounce		

Linear Measures

1 meter	1.09 yards or 3.28 feet or 39.37 inches	1 yard	0.914 meter
1 decimeter (1/10 meter)	3.93 inches	1 foot	0.3048 meter or 3.048 decimeters or 30.48 centimeters
1 centimeter (1/100 meter)	0.39 inch	1 inch	2.54 centimeters or 25.4 millimeters
1 millimeter (1/1000 meter)	0.039 inch		

Contents

This is a **Make-Ahead Buffet** that is as elegant as can be.

Introduction

MAKE PARTY GIVING fun. Don't spend all your time dashing from the kitchen to the table, with last-minute cooking, serving, and clearing the table. Let your guests share the total experience of the party giving—by simply creating a buffet.

Once, party giving was stiff and formal. The printed announcement was followed by a full-dress meal, complete with hand-lettered name cards. The conversation, too, was polite, and at the appropriate time, the men retired to the library or stayed in the dining room for a cigar and a brandy, and the women grouped themselves for a chat.

Fortunately for most of us, those days are gone. Now there is an informality about party giving that is easily translated into a joyful experience. That doesn't mean that there aren't some rules to follow. There are. But they are set up so that the party can flow easily.

One of the biggest drawbacks to a buffet party is what to put out on the sideboard or on the table. This problem—if it is a problem—is solved with any one of the many buffet menus in your **Buffet Entertaining Cookbook.**

There are buffets for all occasions, even one for the children to cook and then set up, as well as many ideas about make-ahead cooking. And buffets for the season—New Year's, Easter, May Day, the indoor or outdoor July 4th bang, and Christmas. And when the company is large, there are specific buffets to take care of the numbers—including a Bridal buffet that sets up food for 16 and a cake for up to 100.

And to complete the buffet, there are a host of beverages, both with and without alcohol. So, enjoy.

Buffets For The Occasion

Your house is large; your apartment is small, you expect ten people to the party, you expect 100 to the wedding; snow covers the sidewalk, the patio is sun-drenched—whatever the circumstance, partytime is a good time for a buffet. And you'll find a wide assortment of special occasion buffets in these pages.

THE MAKE-AHEAD BUFFET

Champagne
Almond Macaroons
Mixed Salted Nuts and Raisins
Smoked Salmon Quiche*
Zucchini and Italian Sausage Quiche*
Avocado, Artichoke and Lettuce Salad,
Italian Dressing
Demitasse Coffee Bar*

THE QUICHE COURSE

The following two quiches are perfect for a Réveillon, that convivial supper traditionally served after midnight mass on Christmas Eve in France and Italy.

Smoked Salmon Quiche

Make-ahead Note: Prebake pastry shell. Chop salmon and shred cheese. Refrigerate all three. One hour before serving, heat oven and fill shell, following recipe from Step 3. OR: Bake quiche early in day and refrigerate. Reheat in moderate oven (350°) for 30 minutes

Prebake shell at 450° for 8 minutes; bake quiche at 450° for 15 minutes, then at 350° for 15 minutes. Makes 8 servings.

1 package piecrust mix
½ pound smoked salmon, chopped
1 cup shredded Swiss cheese (4 ounces)
4 eggs
1 cup milk
½ cup heavy cream
¼ cup grated Parmesan cheese
1 tablespoon finely chopped fresh dill OR:

1 teaspoon dried dill weed
½ teaspoon salt
¼ teaspoon pepper
Red caviar

1 Prepare piecrust mix, following label directions. Roll out to a 14-inch round on a lightly floured surface; fit into a 10-inch (6-cup) fluted quiche dish (or use a 10-inch pie plate). Trim pastry overhang to ½-inch and turn under; flute to make a stand-up edge. Prick shell well over entire surface with a fork.
2 Bake in a hot oven (450°) for 8 minutes; remove to wire rack; cool slightly.
3 Spread salmon evenly over bottom of pastry shell; sprinkle Swiss cheese over salmon.
4 Beat eggs lightly in a medium-size bowl. Add milk, heavy cream, Parmesan cheese, dill, salt and pepper; blend well. Pour into pastry shell.
5 Bake in a hot oven (450°) 15 minutes; lower oven temperature to moderate (350°) and bake 15 minutes or until center is almost firm but still soft. Let stand 15 minutes before serving. Garnish with red caviar and fresh dill, if you wish.

Zucchini and Italian Sausage Quiche

Make-ahead Note: Prebake pastry shell. Cook zucchini and sausage; prepare milk-egg mixture. Shred cheese. Refrigerate all. One hour before serving, heat oven; fill shell, following recipe from Step 5. OR: Bake quiche early in day; let cool and refrigerate. Reheat in moderate oven (350°) for 30 minutes

Prebake pastry shell at 450° for 8 minutes. Bake quiche at 450° for 15 minutes, and then at 350° for 15 minutes. Makes 8 servings.

1 package piecrust mix
1 pound zucchini, shredded (2 cups)
4 tablespoons (½ stick) butter or margarine
5 sweet Italian sausages (½ pound)
1 cup shredded Swiss cheese (4 ounces)
4 eggs
1 cup milk
½ cup heavy cream
¼ cup grated Parmesan cheese
½ teaspoon salt
¼ teaspoon white pepper

(continued)

1 Prepare piecrust mix, following label directions. Roll out to a 14-inch round on a lightly floured surface; fit into a 10-inch (6-cup) fluted quiche dish (or use a 10-inch pie plate). Trim pastry overhang to ½-inch; turn under and flute to make a stand-up edge. Prick shell well over surface with a fork.

2 Bake in a hot oven (450°) for 8 minutes; remove to wire rack; cool slightly.

3 Sauté zucchini in 2 tablespoons of the butter in a large skillet for 5 minutes or until tender. Remove to bowl.

4 Remove casing from 4 sausages and crumble; cut remaining sausage into ½-inch rounds. Cook crumbled sausage and sausage rounds in remaining 2 tablespoons butter in same skillet until no pink remains. Drain on paper toweling.

5 Spread cooked zucchini evenly onto bottom of pastry shell; sprinkle crumbled sausage and Swiss cheese over zucchini.

6 Beat eggs lightly in a large bowl. Add milk, heavy cream, cheese, salt and pepper; blend well. Pour into pastry shell. Arrange sausage rounds around edge of quiche, pressing in slightly.

7 Bake in a hot oven (450°) for 15 minutes; lower oven temperature to moderate (350°) and bake for 15 minutes or until center is almost firm but still soft. Let stand 15 minutes before serving.

DEMITASSE COFFEE BAR

To top off this elegant supper, let your guests personalize their demitasse with some special additions.

Serve a pot of dark, fragrant espresso. Assemble a selection of liqueurs and brandy, perhaps for Cafe Royale, or serve a bowl of softly whipped cream and a shaker of cinnamon for Cappucino.

OPEN-HOUSE BUFFET

Parslied Blue Cheese Spread*
Herbed Cheese Spread*
Ginger-Almond Cheese Spread*
Country Pâté*
Rye Bread/Pumpernickel/Sesame Crackers
Pickled Beets, Onions and Gherkins
Spicy Marinated Shrimp*
Baked Ham Glazed With Port and Apricots*
Cauliflower and Broccoli Almondine
Spirited Fruited Pears*
Coffee

When the occasion is festive, give yourself time to enjoy the party by making the food ahead, as with the **Open-House Buffet**.

THE CHEESE COURSE

These three cheese spreads are served with thick slices of rye or dark pumpernickel bread.

Make-ahead Note: All cheese spreads can be made a day or two in advance and kept refrigerated until ready to serve

Parslied Blue Cheese Spread

This spread features a duet of two cheeses plus herbs and tangy olives

Makes 2 cups.

¼ pound blue cheese, softened
2 packages (3 ounces each) cream cheese, softened
½ cup (1 stick) butter or margarine, softened
⅓ cup chopped pimiento-stuffed green olives
1½ teaspoons chopped chives
¾ cup chopped parsley
1 small clove garlic, minced
1 tablespoon brandy (optional)

1 Combine blue cheese, cream cheese, butter or margarine, olives, chives, 1½ teaspoons of the parsley, garlic and brandy in a medium-size bowl; blend well.

2 Line a 2-cup bowl with plastic wrap. Turn cheese mixture into bowl, packing it down firmly; refrigerate.

3 To serve: Turn cheese ball out onto serving platter. Peel off plastic wrap. Sprinkle with remaining parsley and garnish with pimiento, if you wish.

Herbed Cheese Spread

An up-to-date adaptation of the classic European Liptauer cheese

Makes 2 cups.

1 cup creamed-style cottage cheese
1 cup (2 sticks) butter or margarine, softened
1 tablespoon whole caraway seeds
1 tablespoon drained, chopped capers
1 tablespoon minced chives
1 tablespoon dry mustard
1 tablespoon chopped anchovy fillets
1 tablespoon paprika
½ cup chopped radishes *(continued)*

1 Combine cottage cheese, butter or margarine, caraway seeds, capers, chives, dry mustard, anchovies and paprika; blend well.
2 Line a 2-cup bowl with plastic wrap. Turn cheese mixture into bowl, packing it down firmly; refrigerate.
3 To serve: Turn cheese ball out onto serving platter. Peel off plastic wrap. Garnish with chopped radishes and any remaining anchovies.

Ginger-Almond Cheese Spread

The piquant sweetness of ginger is combined with the crunch of toasted almonds

Makes 3 cups.

2 packages (8 ounces each) cream cheese, softened
1 jar (10 ounces) preserved ginger, drained and finely chopped
2 teaspoons lemon juice
1 cup toasted blanched almonds, chopped

1 Combine cheese and all but 2 tablespoons of the ginger, lemon juice and ¾ cup of the almonds in a medium-size bowl; blend well.
2 Line a 3-cup bowl with plastic wrap. Spoon cheese mixture into bowl, packing it down firmly; refrigerate.
3 To serve: Turn cheese ball out onto serving platter. Peel off plastic wrap. Garnish with reserved ginger and almonds.

Country Pâté

Make-ahead Note: This smooth, mellow pâté can be baked a day or two in advance, and served cold or warmed in a slow oven. Try it spread on dark pumpernickel with a topping of pickled beets or onions

Bake at 350° for 1½ hours.
Makes 16 servings.

1 pound beef liver
¾ pound boneless pork shoulder
¼ pound pork fat back
1 large onion, quartered
3 tablespoons butter or margarine
¼ cup flour
3 teaspoons salt
1 teaspoon ground allspice
¼ teaspoon ground cloves
½ teaspoon pepper
2 cups milk
2 eggs
Crisp bacon strips
Sautéed mushrooms
Watercress or parsley

1 Soak liver in cold water for 30 minutes; pat dry on paper toweling. Trim fat and membranes from liver. Grind liver, pork, pork fat and onion twice through the fine blade of meat grinder. Place in large bowl.
2 Melt butter or margarine in medium-size saucepan; stir in flour, salt, all-spice, cloves and pepper. Gradually add milk. Cook, stirring constantly, until sauce thickens and bubbles 1 minute; cool slightly. Stir hot sauce into ground liver-meat mixture; add eggs and beat with a wooden spoon until thoroughly mixed. Turn mixture into a greased 6-cup shallow baking dish.
3 Place dish in larger pan; pour boiling water into outer pan to come half way up the side of pâté dish.
4 Bake in moderate oven (350°) 1½ hours or until juices run clear when pâté is pierced with a fork or a thin-bladed knife.
5 Remove from water bath and allow to cool; when pâté is room temperature, cover and refrigerate overnight or longer. Garnish with bacon, mushrooms and watercress or parsley.

Spicy Marinated Shrimp

Make-ahead Note: Prepare the marinade a day or so ahead and refrigerate. Party morning: Pour marinade over the warm shrimp right in the serving bowl. Cover and refrigerate

Makes 8 servings.

2 pounds cooked fresh shrimp, peeled and deveined, with tails left on
OR: 1½ pounds cooked frozen, peeled, deveined shrimp
1 large red onion, sliced
2 large lemons, sliced
½ cup olive or vegetable oil
¼ cup wine vinegar
2 tablespoons lemon juice
1 clove garlic, halved
1 bay leaf
1 teaspoon dry mustard
1 teaspoon leaf basil, crumbled
1 teaspoon salt

¼ teaspoon black pepper
3 or 4 whole allspice
Parsley

1 Layer shrimp, red onion and lemon slices in a medium-size bowl.
2 Combine oil, vinegar, lemon juice, garlic, bay leaf, dry mustard, basil, salt, pepper and allspice in a jar with a tight fitting lid; cover; shake thoroughly.
3 Pour marinade over shrimp; toss gently. Cover; refrigerate several hours or overnight, tossing occasionally. Serve with decorative food picks and garnish with parsley sprigs.

HOW TO ORGANIZE A BUFFET

First, start with the menu. If you are to do all the cooking, keep it simple and easy to serve. A meal as plain as a casserole main dish, crisp green salad, ice-cream dessert, and coffee can be made ahead, and needs little last-minute attention. Yet, with a few bright garnishes, it can be quite partylike. It's best not to attempt a dish you have never tried before. Instead, give it a preview for the family. They'll like the surprise and you'll have the practice.

Make up a shopping list. Buy staples ahead, perishables the day before to take advantage of what is freshest in the supermarket.

Post the menu with a cooking schedule. Include what can be done a day or even two ahead, how much time to allow to cook or heat the food, what will need to be done, just before serving time. Then check off each step as you do it.

Check linen, silver, and china. Decide which serving dish to use for each food. If your party is too large for your supply, ask to borrow extras from a friend. On the day of your party, lay out everything, including accessories such as salt and pepper shakers, so they can be moved quickly to your serving spot.

Plan a centerpiece. A fancy flower and candle decoration looks lovely, but a simple bowl of fruit (to double with cheese for dessert) or a bouquet of flowers from your own garden is quite enough.

Save time for yourself. Allow at least an hour before the party to dress leisurely, so you'll be ready to greet your guests, relaxed and eager to enjoy the fun.

Baked Ham Glazed with Port and Apricots

Make-ahead Note: Pairing wine and fruit for a glaze makes this ham special. It can be baked and glazed as early in the day as you wish, for it is good warm or cold. And you can reheat it in a moderate oven, if you wish

Bake at 325° for 2½ hours.
Makes 12 servings.

1 fully cooked ham, weighing 10 to 12 pounds
½ cup apricot preserves
2 tablespoons prepared mustard
⅓ cup ruby port
  Whole canned apricots
  Watercress

1 Place ham on rack in large shallow roasting pan.
2 Bake in slow oven (325°) 1½ hours. Trim off skin, if any, and excess fat.
3 Mix apricot preserves, mustard and wine in small saucepan. Heat slowly, stirring often; brush part over ham.
4 Continue baking, brushing several times with remaining glaze, 1 hour, or until richly glazed. Serve ham hot, or at room temperature. Garnish with apricots and watercress. Serve with a choice of mustard and chutney.

Spirited Pears

Make-ahead Note: The day before the party poach fresh pears in a light syrup with a touch of sweet orange spirits, then chill

Makes 8 servings.

8 firm, ripe pears
¼ cup lemon juice
1½ cups sugar
3 cups water
1 one-inch piece vanilla bean, split
  OR: 1 teaspoon vanilla extract
½ cup mixed candied fruits, chopped
2 tablespoons grated lemon peel
¼ cup orange-flavored liqueur

1 Wash pears. Core each from bottom, keeping pear whole. Pare, leaving stem intact. Brush with part of the lemon juice.
2 Combine sugar, water and vanilla bean in deep skillet or Dutch oven; bring to boiling. Add pears and remaining lemon juice; cover. Simmer

(continued)

over very low heat, turning once or twice until just tender, 10 to 15 minutes. Let pears cool in syrup at least 30 minutes.

3 Measure 2 cups syrup from pears into a large saucepan; bring to boiling. Boil rapidly until reduced to 1 cup; add candied fruits and lemon peel; cook 5 minutes longer. Cool; stir in liqueur.

4 Arrange pears in a shallow baking dish; pour reduced syrup over. Chill, turning pears and basting often with syrup, several times.

5 Serve chilled pears with some of the syrup and candied fruits spooned over. Pass sweetened whipped cream, if you wish.

FIRESIDE BUFFET

Hot Cinnamon Sparkle
Parmesan Crisps
Chicken à l'Orange
Chive Risotto   Casserole Peas
Lotus Salad Bowl
Macaroon Custard Tarts
Coffee

Hot Cinnamon Sparkle

A hot drink that will take the chill out of a winter's eve

Makes 8 servings.

1 can (46 ounces) unsweetened pineapple juice
1 container (3¼ ounces) red cinnamon candies
½ cup bottled grenadine syrup
¼ cup lemon juice

1 Combine pineapple juice, cinnamon candies and grenadine syrup in a medium-size saucepan.

2 Heat, stirring, until candies melt and mixture is hot; stir in lemon juice. Pour into mugs; serve warm.

Parmesan Crisps

Nibble size crisps with a pungent flavor

Bake at 425° for 8 minutes.
Makes about 8 dozen.

1 package piecrust mix
1 envelope Parmesan salad dressing mix
5 tablespoons cold water

1 Combine piecrust mix and dry salad dressing mix in a large bowl. Sprinkle water over top, 1 tablespoon at a time; mix lightly with a fork.

2 Roll out, half at a time, ⅛ inch thick, on a lightly floured pastry cloth or board; cut into 1½-inch rounds with a plain or fluted cutter. Place on a large cookie sheet.

3 Bake in hot oven (425°) 8 minutes, or until golden. Serve warm or cold.

Chicken à l'Orange

Boneless chicken breasts are smothered in an orange sauce for a taste treat you won't forget

Bake at 350° for 1 hour.
Makes 8 servings.

8 boneless chicken breasts, weighing about 10 ounces each

Wintertime means let's-stay-in time, and when you do, surprise the family with this **Fireside Buffet.**

⅓ cup sifted all-purpose flour
1½ teaspoons salt
 1 teaspoon garlic powder
 ½ teaspoon paprika
 ⅓ cup sliced almonds
 5 tablespoons butter or margarine
 1 can (6 ounces) frozen concentrated orange
   juice
1½ cups water
 1 teaspoon leaf rosemary, crumbled
 ¼ teaspoon leaf thyme, crumbled
 2 tablespoons cornstarch
   CHIVE RISOTTO (recipe follows)

1 Coat chicken with a mixture of flour, 1 tea-spoon salt, garlic powder and paprika.
2 Sauté almonds in butter or margarine until golden in a large frying pan; remove from pan. Brown chicken breasts in drippings in same pan; place in a single layer in a baking pan, 13x9x2. Pour all drippings from pan.
3 Stir orange-juice concentrate, water, rose-mary, thyme and ½ teaspoon salt into pan. Heat to boiling; pour over chicken; cover.
4 Bake in moderate oven (350°) 1 hour, or until chicken is tender. Remove to another pan; keep warm. Reheat liquid in baking pan to boiling; thicken with cornstarch.
5 Spoon CHIVE RISOTTO onto a large serving platter; arrange chicken over rice; sprinkle with almonds. Serve sauce separately to spoon over chicken.

CHIVE RISOTTO

Sauté 2½ cups packaged enriched precooked rice in 3 tablespoons butter or margarine, stir-ring constantly, until golden in a large frying pan. Drain liquid from 2 cans (3 or 4 ounces each) chopped mushrooms into a 4-cup mea-sure; add water to make 2½ cups. Stir into rice with mushrooms, 3 envelopes instant chicken broth, and ¼ cup cut chives. Heat to boiling; cover; remove from heat. Let stand 10 minutes. Makes 8 servings.

Casserole Peas

Popular go-alongs with the chicken

Bake at 350° for 25 minutes.
Makes 8 servings.

 1 envelope blue cheese salad dressing mix
 1 teaspoon sugar
 ¼ cup lemon juice
 2 tablespoons water
 ⅔ cup vegetable oil
 1 large head romaine

 1 bunch watercress
 2 packages (10 ounces each) frozen peaches,
   thawed and drained
 2 cups seedless green grapes
 1 can (5 ounces) water chestnuts, sliced

1 Combine dressing mix, sugar, lemon juice and water in a jar with a tight lid; shake well. Add vegetable oil; shake again. Set aside.
2 Line a large salad bowl with romaine leaves; break remainder in bite-size pieces and place in bottom. Pull leaves from watercress; discard stems.
3 Arrange watercress, peach slices and grapes in rings around edge in bowl; overlap water chestnuts in center.
4 Pour about ½ cup salad dressing over all; toss lightly. Serve with additional dressing.

Lotus Salad Bowl

Fresh lettuce and watercress are tossed with a blue cheese dressing

Makes 8 servings.

 3 packages (8 ounces each) frozen green
   peas with cream sauce
 3 tablespoons butter or margarine
2¼ cups milk
 1 cup crunchy nutlike cereal nuggets
 1 package (4 ounces) shredded Cheddar
   cheese

1 Prepare peas with butter or margarine and milk, following label directions. Mix cereal and cheese in a bowl; set aside ½ cup.
2 Layer one third of the peas into a 7-cup bak-ing dish; sprinkle with half of the remaining cereal mixture. Repeat layers. Spoon remaining peas on top; sprinkle with the ½ cup cereal mixture.
3 Bake in moderate oven (350°) 25 minutes, or until bubbly and topping is lightly toasted.

Macaroon Custard Tarts

Delicate tarts with a rich custard-fruit filling

Bake shells at 425° for 15 minutes.
Makes 6 servings.

 ½ package piecrust mix
 1 package (3 ounces) egg-custard mix

(continued)

1⅓ cups milk
1 cup thawed frozen whipped topping
½ cup macaroon crumbs
  Mandarin-orange segments, well drained

1 Prepare piecrust mix, following label directions, or make pastry from your favorite single-crust recipe. Roll out, ⅛ inch thick, on a lightly floured pastry cloth or board. Cut into 4½-inch rounds; fit each into a 3-inch tart-shell pan. Prick shells well all over with a fork. Set pans in a jelly-roll pan for easy handling.
2 Bake in hot oven (425°) 15 minutes, or until golden. Cool completely in pans on a wire rack.
3 Prepare custard mix with the 1⅓ cups milk, following label directions; pour into a medium-size bowl. Set bowl in a pan of ice and water to speed cooling. Chill, stirring several times, until completely cold; fold in whipped topping and macaroon crumbs. Spoon into tart shells.
4 Chill several hours, or until firm. Just before serving, garnish each tart with a rosette of mandarin-orange segments.

THE BOWL GAME BUFFET

Continental Meatballs*
Roast Turkey Breast with Barbecue Sauce*
Arkansas Pecan Dressing*
Chilled Shrimp   Red Cocktail Sauce
Cold Meat Platter: Sliced ham,
salami, bologna, cheese
Tuna Salad   Green Salad
Potato Salad   Cole Slaw
Concorde Salad*   Deviled Eggs
Scalloped Potatoes*
Cold raw vegetable platter: Cauliflowerets,
carrot sticks, radishes, turnip chunks,
green pepper strips, celery stalks
Cheese Dip   Bacon-horseradish Dip
Carrot Cake*
Double-Frosted Bourbon Brownies*
Coffee   Beer   Soft Drinks

Continental Meatballs

The Italian influence is dominant in these oregano-seasoned meatballs

Makes 10 to 12 servings.

2 pounds ground chuck
1 pound ground pork
2 cups soft bread crumbs (4 slices)

1 large onion, finely chopped (1 cup)
1 cup finely chopped green pepper
2 tablespoons dried parsley flakes
2 tablespoons leaf oregano, crumbled
3 teaspoons salt
2½ teaspoons garlic powder
2 eggs
3 tablespoons vegetable oil
2 cans (1 pound each) stewed tomatoes
1 can (6 ounces) tomato paste
¾ cup water

1 Mix chuck and pork with bread crumbs, onion, pepper, parsley flakes, oregano, salt, 2 teaspoons of the garlic powder and eggs until well blended; shape into bite-size meatballs using 1 rounded teaspoon of mixture for each (makes about 120 meatballs).
2 Heat oil in large skillet; add meatballs, about one-fourth at a time, and brown on all sides; remove with slotted spoon to a Dutch oven.
3 Add tomatoes, tomato paste, water and remaining ½ teaspoon garlic powder to skillet; bring to boiling, stirring and crushing tomatoes with wooden spoon; lower heat; cover. Simmer 20 minutes; pour over meatballs in Dutch oven. Simmer, covered, 40 minutes.

Roast Turkey Breast with Barbecue Sauce

This easy-to-carve, all white meat keeps warm for hours

Roast at 325° for 3 to 3½ hours.
Makes about 8 servings.

1 turkey breast (8 to 9 pounds), defrosted
3 tablespoons butter or margarine, softened
BARBECUE SAUCE (recipe follows)

1 Place turkey breast, skin side up, on rack in shallow open roasting pan. Rub skin well with butter or margarine. Insert roast thermometer in thick part of breast, not touching bone.
2 Roast in a moderate oven (325°) for 2½ hours, basting frequently with drippings.
3 Brush with Barbecue Sauce and continue to roast, brushing occasionally with sauce, 1 to 1½ hours longer or until juices run yellow when breast is pierced with a fork. Roast thermometer should register 180°.
Note: Turkey can be removed from oven when done, and covered with foil to keep warm while potatoes and dressing bake.

Barbecue Sauce

Makes about 2 cups.

⅓ cup chopped onion
2 cloves garlic, minced
2 tablespoons vegetable oil
1 jar (12 ounces) apricot preserves
¼ cup chili sauce
⅓ cup wine vinegar
1 teaspoon hickory salt

Sauté onion and garlic in oil in a small saucepan until soft. Stir in preserves, chili sauce, vinegar and salt. Simmer for approximately 20 minutes.

Arkansas Pecan Dressing

A delicious dressing that will disappear fast

Bake at 375° for 30 minutes.
Makes about 8 servings.

1 cup chopped celery
1 cup chopped green pepper
1 large onion, chopped (1 cup)
½ cup (1 stick) butter or margarine
½ cup chopped parsley
1½ teaspoons poultry seasoning
1 tablespoon ground sage
1 package (16 ounces) cornbread stuffing mix
4 cups whole wheat bread crumbs (about 8 slices)
2 cups chicken broth
½ cup chopped pecans

1 Sauté celery, green pepper and onion in butter or margarine in a large skillet until soft. Stir in parsley, poultry seasoning, sage, cornbread stuffing mix, whole wheat crumbs and chicken broth. Stir to mix thoroughly; stir in pecans. Spoon into a buttered 12-cup baking dish.
2 Bake in a moderate oven (375°) for 30 minutes.

Concorde Salad

This tangy salad improves on standing in the refrigerator

Makes about 8 servings.

1 can (1 pound) French-style green beans
1 can (1 pound) tiny peas

1 stalk celery, chopped (2 cups)
½ cup chopped green pepper
1 can (4 ounces) pimientos, diced
1 medium-size onion, sliced in rings
½ to 1 cup sugar
¾ cup cider vinegar
½ cup vegetable oil
1 teaspoon salt

1 Drain beans and peas and combine with celery, green pepper, pimientos and onion in a large bowl. Stir sugar, vinegar, oil and salt together in a 2-cup measure until sugar is dissolved.
2 Pour mixture over vegetables; stir gently. Refrigerate 24 hours.
3 Drain liquid off 30 minutes before serving.
Note: For a less sweet salad, use the smaller amount of sugar.

Scalloped Potatoes

Creamy smooth with an attractively browned surface, this is everyone's favorite

Bake at 375° for 1 hour.
Makes 6 to 8 servings.

6 to 8 potatoes (about 3 pounds)
3 large onions, sliced thin
3 tablespoons flour
1½ teaspoons salt
¼ teaspoon pepper
2 cups milk, scalded
2 tablespoons butter or margarine

1 Pare and slice potatoes very thinly; parboil in boiling salted water in large saucepan 3 minutes; drain.
2 Layer potatoes and onions in a 10-cup baking dish, sprinkling flour, salt and pepper between layers; pour milk over potatoes; dot with butter or margarine; cover.
3 Bake in a moderate oven (375°) for 45 minutes; uncover. Bake 15 minutes longer or until potatoes are tender and top is browned slightly.
Note: For creamier potatoes, add ½ cup scalded cream the last 5 or 10 baking minutes.

Sandwiched between Christmas and New Year's is bowl-game time, and this means snack food—unless you watch the game while eating **The Bowl Game Buffet.**

Carrot Cake

Here's a moist, spicy cake that needs no frosting

Bake at 325° for 1 hour and 20 minutes.
Makes one 10-inch tube cake.

3⅓ cups sifted all-purpose flour
 2 cups sugar
 1 teaspoon baking powder
 1 teaspoon baking soda
 1 teaspoon salt
 1 teaspoon ground nutmeg
 2 teaspoons ground cinnamon
 4 eggs
1½ cups vegetable oil
 2 teaspoons vanilla
 2 cups finely shredded raw carrots
 1 cup chopped walnuts

1 Sift flour, sugar, baking powder, baking soda, salt, nutmeg and cinnamon into large bowl; make a well in center. Add eggs, oil and vanilla; beat with wooden spoon until smooth. Stir in carrots and walnuts. Turn mixture into a 10-inch greased Bundt or angel cake tube pan.
2 Bake in a slow oven (325°) for 1 hour and 20 minutes, or until top springs back when lightly pressed with fingertip.
3 Cook cake in baking pan on wire rack for 10 minutes. Remove cake from the pan. Cool completely before cutting. Wrap in plastic wrap to ensure adequate storage.

Double-Frosted Bourbon Brownies

It's best to make a double batch and freeze what's left—they disappear fast!

Bake at 325° for 30 minutes.
Makes about 3 dozen squares.

¾ cup sifted all-purpose flour
¼ teaspoon baking soda
¼ teaspoon salt
½ cup sugar
⅓ cup vegetable shortening
 2 tablespoons water
 1 package (6 ounces) semisweet chocolate
   pieces
 1 teaspoon vanilla
 2 eggs
1½ cups coarsely chopped walnuts
 4 tablespoons bourbon
   White Frosting (recipe follows)
   Chocolate Glaze (recipe follows)

1 Sift flour, baking soda and salt onto wax paper.
2 Combine sugar, shortening and water in a medium-size saucepan. Heat, stirring constantly, until sugar melts and mixture comes to boiling. Remove from heat; stir in chocolate pieces and vanilla until smooth.
3 Beat in eggs, one at a time. Stir in flour mixture and walnuts. Spread evenly in 9x9x2-inch greased pan.
4 Bake in a moderate oven (325°) for 30 minutes or until shiny and firm on top. Remove from oven; sprinkle bourbon over top; cool completely.
5 Spread White Frosting evenly over top; chill until firm. Spread Chocolate Glaze over frosting; chill. Cut into squares. Keep refrigerated until ready to serve.

White Frosting

½ cup (1 stick) butter or margarine, softened
 1 teaspoon vanilla or rum extract
 1 cups 10X (confectioners') sugar

Beat butter or margarine and vanilla or rum in a medium-size bowl until creamy; gradually beat in 10X (confectioners') sugar until the mixture has become smooth and spreadable.

CHOCOLATE GLAZE
Combine 1 package (6 ounces) semisweet chocolate pieces and 1 tablespoon vegetable shortening in the top of a double boiler. Set over hot, not boiling, water until melted.

EARLY FALL BUFFET

Cider Cheese Spread
Winter Pear Pâté
Shrimp Bisque
Orange-Glazed Corn Beef Platter
Italian Chicken Bake
Vegetables Amandine
Rosette Fruit Salad
Corn-Biscuit Puffs
Frosted Fruit Fingers
Coffee   Tea

Cider Cheese Spread

An apple-shaped cheese spread

Makes about 3 cups.

1 package (8 ounces) cream cheese
½ cup apple cider
½ pound Swiss cheese, shredded (2 cups)
½ pound Cheddar cheese, shredded (2 cups)
½ cup (1 stick) butter or margarine, melted
  Paprika

1 Beat cream cheese until smooth in a large bowl. Slowly beat in cider, Swiss cheese, Cheddar cheese, and melted butter or margarine; continue beating until fluffy. Pack into a buttered 3-cup bowl, mounding top. Chill overnight until very firm.
2 Several hours before serving, loosen cheese around edge with a knife; invert onto a cutting board or plate. With a small sharp knife, trim away edge of cheese to round shape like an apple; press a stem from a fresh apple into top. Dust cheese all over with paprika.
3 Place on a larger serving plate. For best flavor, let stand at room temperature at least 30 minutes before serving. Garnish with parsley, if you wish, and serve with party-size rye bread and crisp crackers.
Day-before note: This spread keeps well and can be made as many as two or three days ahead. Carve mold into apple shape a day ahead, if you wish, then wrap tightly and chill.

Winter Pear Pâté

This may look like a pear, but the shape and the stem come from the creative cook

Makes about 3 cups.

1 pound chicken livers
1 medium-size onion, chopped (½ cup)
2 cups (4 sticks) butter or margarine
1 envelope instant chicken broth or 1 teaspoon granulated chicken bouillon
1 tablespoon Worcestershire sauce
½ cup sliced pimiento-stuffed olives
  Chopped parsley

1 Rinse chicken livers; cut each into two or three pieces, discarding any fat.
2 Combine livers, onion, 2 sticks of the butter or margarine, chicken broth, and Worcestershire sauce in a medium-size frying pan. Cook

slowly, stirring several times, 10 minutes, or until no pink remains.
3 Spoon mixture into an electric-blender container; cover. Beat until smooth.
4 Melt remaining 2 sticks butter or margarine in a small saucepan; slowly beat into liver mixture until well-blended. Cool, then stir in olives. Pack into a buttered 3-cup bowl. Chill overnight until very firm.
5 Several hours before serving, loosen pâté around edge with a knife; invert onto a cutting board or plate. With a small sharp knife, trim away edge to make a pear shape; press trimmings on top to make stem end of pear; press a stem from a fresh pear into top. Pat parsley all over pâté to cover generously.
6 Place on a large serving plate. Serve with party-size rye bread and crisp crackers.
Day-before note: Making at least one day ahead is a must so pâté will be firm enough to shape. Carve mold into pear shape and coat with parsley several hours ahead, then wrap tightly and keep chilled.

Shrimp Bisque

A quick-fix bisque that is mouth-wateringly good

Makes 16 servings.

1 small onion, minced (¼ cup)
2 tablespoons butter or margarine
3 cans (10¾ ounces each) condensed cream of shrimp soup
3 cups milk
1 can (10¾ ounces) condensed tomato soup
1 envelope instant chicken broth or 1 teaspoon granulated chicken bouillon
¼ teaspoon liquid red pepper seasoning
3 tablespoons lemon juice
2 cups light cream or table cream
3 thin lemon slices

Deceive the eye with these mock fruits made from
Cider Cheese Spread.

1 Sauté onion in butter or margarine until soft in a kettle. Stir in shrimp soup and milk. Heat slowly, stirring several times, just until hot. (As soup heats, pick out several shrimps and set them aside for garnish.)
2 Stir in tomato soup, chicken broth, red pepper seasoning, and lemon juice. Heat until bubbly.
3 Stir in cream; heat just until hot. (Do not boil.)
4 Pour into a tureen. Place saved shrimps on lemon slices; float on top of bisque. Serve in mugs.
Day-before note: Prepare bisque through Step 2; cover and chill. Just before party-time, reheat soup slowly and stir in cream.

Orange-Glazed Corned Beef

Set this up as the star of your early fall buffet

Bake at 325° for 3 hours.
Makes 16 servings.

2 corned-beef oven roasts, weighing about 3 pounds each
⅓ cup dark corn syrup
⅓ cup thawed frozen concentrate for orange-grapefruit juice
JELLIED MUSTARD CREAM *(recipe follows)*

1 Remove roasts from wrappers; place, not touching, on a rack in a shallow baking pan. Do not add water or cover.
2 Bake in slow oven (325°) 2½ hours.
3 Blend corn syrup and orange-grapefruit concentrate in a small bowl; brush part over roasts.
4 Continue baking, brushing every 10 minutes with remaining syrup mixture, 30 minutes, or until meat is fork-tender and richly glazed. Place roasts on a plate; cool, cover, and chill.
5 When ready to serve, slice corned beef ¼ inch thick. Unmold JELLIED MUSTARD CREAM onto each of two large serving platters; overlap corned-beef slices around molds. Frame molds with lettuce and radish roses, if you wish.
JELLIED MUSTARD CREAM—Combine 1 envelope unflavored gelatin and ½ cup water in a small saucepan. Heat slowly, stirring constantly, until gelatin dissolves; pour into a medium-size bowl. Beat in ½ cup mayonnaise or salad dressing and ¼ cup prepared mustard. Chill, stirring several times, until as thick as unbeaten egg white. While gelatin mixture chills, beat ½ cup cream for whipping until stiff in a small bowl; fold into mustard mixture until no streaks of white remain. Pour into 2 one-cup molds. Chill until firm. Makes about 2 cups.

JELLIED MUSTARD CREAM

Combine 1 envelope unflavored gelatin and ½ cup water in a small saucepan. Heat slowly, stirring constantly, until gelatin dissolves; pour into a medium-size bowl. Beat in ½ cup mayonnaise or salad dressing and ¼ cup prepared mustard. Chill, stirring several times, until as thick as unbeaten egg white. While gelatin mixture chills, beat ½ cup cream for whipping until stiff in a small bowl; fold into mustard mixture until no streaks of white remain. Pour into 2 one-cup molds. Chill until firm. Makes about 2 cups.
Day-before note: Roast corned beef and chill overnight, ready to slice an hour or so before partytime. Make mustard molds the day before, too.

Italian Chicken Bake

A slice of corned beef and a spoonful of this casserole, and you'll know why a buffet table is known as a groaning table

Bake at 350° for 30 minutes.
Makes 16 servings.

3 broiler-fryers, weighing about 3 pounds each, cut up
1 medium-size onion, peeled and sliced
2½ teaspoons salt
½ teaspoon peppercorns
1 pound mushrooms, trimmed and sliced
1 cup (2 sticks) butter or margarine
1 cup fine soft bread crumbs
½ sifted all-purpose flour
¼ teaspoon pepper
¼ teaspoon ground nutmeg
2 cups light cream or table cream
½ cup dry sherry
1 package (1 pound) thin spaghetti, broken in 2-inch lengths
1 cup grated Parmesan cheese

1 Combine chicken, onion, 1 teaspoon of the salt, peppercorns, and enough water to cover in a kettle. Heat to boiling; cover. Cook 40 minutes, or until chicken is tender. Remove from broth and cool until easy to handle. Strain broth into a 4-cup measure and set aside for making sauce.
2 Pull skin from chicken and take meat from bones; cube meat; place in a large bowl.
3 Sauté mushrooms in ¼ cup of the butter or margarine until soft in a large frying pan; combine with chicken.
4 Melt remaining butter or margarine in a large

saucepan. Measure out ¼ cup and toss with bread crumbs in a small bowl; set aside.

5 Stir flour, remaining 1½ teaspoons salt, pepper, and nutmeg into remaining butter or margarine in saucepan; cook, stirring constantly, until bubbly. Stir in 3½ cups of the chicken broth and cream. Continue cooking and stirring until sauce thickens and boils 1 minute; remove from heat. Stir in sherry.

6 While sauce cooks, cook spaghetti, following label directions; drain well. Spoon into two baking dishes, 13x9x2. Spoon chicken mixture over spaghetti; spoon sauce over all.

7 Add Parmesan cheese to bread-crumb mixture; toss lightly to mix. Sprinkle over mixture in baking dishes.

8 Bake in moderate oven (350°) 30 minutes, or until bubbly and crumb topping is toasted. Garnish with bouquets of watercress, sliced mushrooms, and pimiento strips, if you wish.

Day-before note: Fix casseroles through Step 7; cover and chill. About an hour before serving, remove from refrigerator and uncover. Bake in moderate oven (350°) 40 minutes, or until bubbly. If casseroles must stand a bit before serving, leave in oven with heat turned off.

Vegetables Amandine

The French word for almonds is amandé—'tho this is a cosmopolitan dish

Makes 16 servings.

½ cup sliced almonds
3 packages (9 ounces each) frozen Italian green beans
3 cans (1 pound each) whole carrots
½ cup (1 stick) butter or margarine
1 tablespoon lemon juice
½ teaspoon salt
¼ teaspoon pepper

1 Place almonds in a small frying pan; heat very slowly, shaking pan constantly, until almonds are toasted. Remove from heat.

2 Cook green beans in a large saucepan, following label directions; drain; keep warm. Heat carrots in their liquid in a second large saucepan; drain; keep warm.

3 Melt butter or margarine over medium heat in a medium-size frying pan; continue heating, shaking pan often, 2 to 3 minutes, or until butter foams up and turns golden-brown. (Watch carefully, for it turns quickly.) Remove pan from heat; stir in lemon juice, salt, and pepper.

4 Spoon half of the beans and carrots in separate sections in each of two heated serving bowls. Drizzle half of the butter mixture over each; sprinkle with almonds.

Day-before note: Vegetables cook or heat quickly, so there's little fixing ahead here. However, to save last-minute fuss, toast the almonds the day before and store in a tightly covered container.

Rosette Fruit Salad

The combination of fruits and vegetables will gladden the eye as well as the palate

Makes 16 servings.

1 large head iceberg lettuce, trimmed and chopped
1 medium-size head chicory or curly endive, trimmed and chopped
2 large red eating apples, halved, cored and sliced
2 large stalks celery, trimmed and sliced diagonally
2 large seedless grapefruits, pared and sectioned
1 can (1 pound) cling-peach slices, drained
¼ cup vegetable oil
¼ cup honey
¼ cup orange juice
2 tablespoons lemon juice
1 tablespoon poppy seeds

1 Mix lettuce and chicory in a large bowl; place half in each of two large salad bowls.

2 Arrange half of the apple slices, celery, and grapefruit sections in rings on top of each; place peach slices in rosettes in centers.

3 Combine vegetable oil, honey, orange and lemon juices, and poppy seeds in a jar with a tight lid; shake well to mix.

4 Just before serving, pour half of the dressing over each salad; toss lightly to mix.

Day-before note: Wash lettuce and chicory, dry well, and chop. Place in a large transparent bag and chill. Slice celery and section grapefruits; place in separate containers, cover, and chill. Mix dressing and chill. To prevent apples from darkening, slice them just before you're ready to arrange salads at partytime.

Corn-Biscuit Puffs

Feathery light rolls to accompany the meat

Bake at 400° for 15 minutes.
Makes 30 puffs.

2 packages (9 ounces each) corn-muffin mix
2 cups biscuit mix
2 eggs
1½ cups milk

1 Grease 30 large muffin-pan cups lightly, or place foil baking cups in pans.
2 Combine corn-muffin and biscuit mixes in a large bowl; add eggs and milk all at once. Stir mixture until evenly moist, then beat ½ minute. (Batter may still be slightly lumpy.) Spoon into prepared muffin-pan cups.
3 Bake in hot oven (400°) 15 minutes, or until golden. Remove from muffin cups; cool slightly on wire racks. Serve warm.
Day-before note: Bake rolls ahead, then reheat before partytime. Place rolls in a large brown paper bag; close bag; sprinkle bag with a few drops water. Heat in moderate oven (350°) 5 to 10 minutes.

Frosted Fruit Fingers

These fingers with a hot or cold beverage round out any fall buffet

Bake at 325° for 45 minutes.
Makes 30 little cakes.

2½ cups sifted cake flour
1 teaspoon baking powder
¾ cup vegetable shortening
1 cup granulated sugar
4 eggs
1 tablespoon grated lemon rind
1 tablespoon lemon juice
¾ cup milk
½ cup golden raisins
½ cup candied lemon peel, chopped
1 cup candied cherries, halved
¼ cup chopped pistachio nuts
½ cup (1 stick) butter or margarine
1 package (1 pound) 10X (confectioners' powdered) sugar, sifted
¼ cup apricot brandy
Green food coloring

1 Grease a baking pan, 15x10x1; line bottom with foil; grease foil.

2 Sift flour and baking powder onto wax paper.
3 Cream shortening and granulated sugar in large bowl of electric mixer. Add eggs and lemon rind; beat at high speed until fluffy-light.
4 Beat in flour mixture, a third at a time, alternately with lemon juice and milk, beating at low speed just until blended. Stir in raisins, lemon peel, cherries, and nuts. Spread evenly in prepared pan.
5 Bake in slow oven (325°) 45 minutes, or until top springs back when lightly pressed with fingertip. Cool completely in pan on a wire rack. Loosen cake around edges with a knife; invert onto a large wire rack; peel off foil.
6 Cream butter or margarine with half of the 10X sugar until fluffy in a medium-size bowl. Blend in remaining 10X sugar, alternately with apricot brandy, until smooth and creamy. Beat in a few drops food coloring to tint pale green.
7 Cut cake in quarters crosswise; stack each two quarters with about ½ cup of the frosting between layers. Spread remaining frosting on tops of cakes. Let stand until frosting is firm. Cut each cake in thirds lengthwise, then each strip in about-2-inch lengths.
Day-before note: Bake cake one or two days ahead, if you wish. Cut in layers and wrap tightly to prevent drying. Frost cakes the day before, but wait to cut them into serving-size pieces until just before partytime.

TEENS' PAJAMA BUFFET

Assorted Dips and Dunks
Crunchy Vegetable Sticks
Chips and Crackers
A-Okay Lasagna
Zigzag Parmesan Loaves
Strawberry Wonder Torts
Assorted Soft Drinks

A-Okay Lasagna

You can slice and butter bread ahead, then pop in to heat along with lasagna

Bake at 350° for 10 minutes.
Makes 12 servings.

CRUST
1 package active dry yeast
¾ cup warm water
2 tablespoons vegetable oil
2 cups sifted all-purpose flour
1 teaspoon salt

Fill a plate with **A-Okay Lasagna, Zigzag Parmesan Loaves, Crunchy Vegetable Sticks,** and chips, for a treat that any teenager will jump at.

FILLING

2 pounds ground beef
2 cans (about 10 ounces each) pizza sauce
4 medium-size onions, sliced and separated into rings
½ cup (1 stick) butter or margarine
6 medium-size potatoes, pared and sliced thin (about 2 pounds)
½ cup water
2 teaspoons salt
2 teaspoons mixed Italian herbs
¼ teaspoon pepper
2 cups (1 pound) cottage cheese
1 can (1 pound) cut green beans, drained
2 eggs, slightly beaten
1 package (8 ounces) sliced mozzarella or pizza cheese, cut into thin strips

1 Make crust: Dissolve yeast in warm water in medium-size bowl; stir in vegetable oil; beat in flour and salt.
2 Turn out onto lightly floured pastry cloth or board; knead 10 times, or until smooth.
3 Place dough in greased medium-size bowl; cover with clean towel; let rise in warm place, away from draft, 30 minutes, or until double in bulk.
4 While dough is rising, make filling: Press ground beef into a large patty in large frying pan; brown 10 minutes; cut into quarters; turn; brown 10 minutes on second side, then break up into chunks; stir in pizza sauce.
5 Sauté onion rings in butter or margarine just until soft in large saucepan; stir in potatoes and water. Mix salt, Italian herbs and pepper in cup; sprinkle half over potatoes. (Save remaining for next step.) Cover; cook 15 minutes, or just until potatoes are tender and water is evaporated.
6 Mix cottage cheese, green beans, eggs and saved seasonings in medium-size bowl.
7 Punch raised dough down; roll out to a large rectangle, 19x15, on lightly floured pastry cloth or board; fit into a greased baking dish, 13x9x2; trim overhang to ½ inch; turn under and flute.
8 Layer half each of potato, cheese and meat mixtures into dish; repeat, ending with meat mixture. Arrange cheese strips to form squares on top.
9 Bake in hot oven (400°) 45 minutes, or until browned and bubbly hot. Let stand about 10 minutes to set, then cut into squares and lift

(continued)

out with wide spatula. (Casserole may be fixed and baked the morning of the party, then chilled. Remove from refrigerator about 1½ hours before partytime, let stand 30 minutes, then reheat in moderate oven [350°] 1 hour, or until hot in middle.)

Zigzag Parmesan Loaves

You can slice and butter bread ahead, then pop in to heat along with lasagna

Bake at 350° for 10 minutes.
Makes 12 servings

2 long loaves Italian bread
½ cup (1 stick) butter or margarine, melted
½ cup grated Parmesan cheese

1 Cut loaves into V-shaped slices ½-inch thick, cutting from outside toward middle and through bottom crust. (Keep slices in order.)
2 Combine melted butter or margarine and cheese. Brush generously over each bread slice; thread slices onto 2 long skewers to re-form into loaves; wrap in foil.
3 Bake in moderate oven (350°) 10 minutes or until heated through. Unwrap loaves and serve on skewers.

WINE AND CHEESE BUFFET

Brandy Pate*
Gallic Cheese Ball*
Assorted Cheese Board*
Your Own French Bread*
Assorted Crackers*
Onion Mustard
Sweet Butter or Margarine
Red and Yellow Delicious Apples
Winter Pears
Empress and Tokay Grapes
Madeira Cake*
Sherry   Madeira
Marzipan

WINES

The choice of wines should depend on guests' preferences, and the availability of particular varieties in local wine shops. The list below provides a few suggestions that are best known and widely available. To serve 16 people, plan on half a fifth-size bottle per guest, choosing eight wines in all, some white and some red.

Pouilly-Fuissé	*White Burgundy*
Mountain Rhine	*White Riesling*
Pink Chablis	*Rosé*
Gamay	*Gamay Beaujolais*
Red Bordeau	*Cabernet*
Red Burgundy	*Pinot Noir*

Just for fun, you might test the group's wine knowledge by pouring wine into decanters, or covering the bottle labels with white napkins. Remember to open the bottles of red wine at least 1 hour before serving to allow them to "breathe". Let white and rosé wines chill at least 4 hours, and keep them chilled until just before serving in ice filled coolers.

Brandy Pâté

You can make it in 15 minutes: best if allowed to mellow a day or two

Makes 12 servings.

1 can (6 ounces) sliced mushrooms
1 envelope unflavored gelatin
⅓ cup brandy
1 roll (8 ounces) liverwurst
1 teaspoon onion salt

1 Drain liquid from mushrooms into a small saucepan; sprinkle gelatin over; stir to soften gelatin; heat slowly, just until gelatin dissolves; stir in brandy.
2 Pour ¼ cup into a 3-cup metal bowl or mold and place in freezer 5 minutes, or until gelatin begins to thicken.
3 Add remaining liquid to a container of an electric blender; cut liverwurst into blender and add mushrooms and onion salt; cover and blend on high speed until very smooth.
4 Swirl thickened gelatin in bowl to coat side; pour pâté mixture in; cover with plastic wrap; chill at least 4 hours. (Pâté is better if it mellows a day or two.)
5 Unmold by running a small knife around edge of bowl; dip bowl into very hot water for a few seconds; invert bowl onto serving plate. Surround with melba toast rounds, thin slices of French bread or rye wafers.

As each guest brings a wine or cheese sample to a **Wine and Cheese Buffet**, go all out with a knock-out centerpiece and a wide assortment of fruits.

Gallic Cheese Ball

A pungent blend of cream cheese, garlic, pepper and herb-blended salt—so like the expensive French import

Makes 12 servings.

2 packages (8 ounces each) cream cheese, softened
¼ cup dairy sour cream
1 clove garlic, mashed
1 tablespoon herb-blended salt
¼ teaspoon seasoned pepper

1 Beat cream cheese until very smooth in a medium-size bowl; mix in sour cream, garlic, herb-blended salt and pepper until well blended. Chill mixture at least 1 hour.
2 Shape mixture into a 4-inch ball on a flat plate; cover with plastic wrap. Chill until serving time. (This can be done up to a week before serving.)
To serve: Slide a wide pancake turner under cheese ball and transfer to serving tray. Surround with an assortment of crisp crackers. Garnish ball with a "bow" of thin strips of pimiento, if you wish.

CHEESE BOARD
Choose 8 from the following list of cheeses and buy between ½ to 1 pound for each variety.

Sharp Cheddar	Monterey Jack
Port Salut	Bonbel
Edam	Gouda
Brie	Camembert
Jarlsberg	Swiss
Blue	Roquefort

Remove cheeses from their wrappings and let them stand at room temperature for about 1 hour before party time. (Cheeses reach their flavor peak at room temperature.) Allow enough room between varieties on cheese board for guests to cut off slices easily. Or, you might use several cheese boards, separating the milder-flavored cheeses from the stronger varieties. After the party, wrap any leftover cheeses individually in plastic wrap or aluminum foil and refrigerate as soon as possible.

Your Own French Bread

Slice a whole loaf, then reshape it as a loaf on a wooden board, serving one loaf at a time

Bake at 450° for 15 minutes,
then at 350° for 30 minutes.
Makes 3 long loaves.

1 envelope active dry yeast
2 cups very warm water
6½ cups all-purpose flour
2 tablespoons sugar
1 tablespoon salt
 Cornmeal
1 egg white, beaten

1 Sprinkle yeast and 1 teaspoon sugar into very warm water in large bowl. (The water should feel comfortably warm when dropped on wrist.) Stir until yeast dissolves. Allow to stand 10 minutes, or until mixture bubbles.
2 Stir in 2 cups of the flour and the sugar and salt until mixture is smooth; gradually beat in enough of remaining 4½ cups flour to make a stiff dough.
3 Turn out onto lightly-floured pastry cloth or board; knead dough about 5 minutes, or until smooth and elastic, adding only enough flour to keep dough from sticking.
4 Place dough in a large greased bowl; turn to coat all over with shortening; cover with clean towel. Let rise in warm place, away from draft, 45 minutes, or until double in bulk.
5 Punch dough down; cover; let rise again 30 minutes, or until double in bulk.
6 Punch dough down; knead 1 minute on lightly-floured pastry board; divide in thirds. Roll out, one at a time, to a 15x10-inch rectangle. Roll up tightly from long side, jelly-roll fashion; pinch long seam tightly to seal. Roll loaf gently back and forth with hands to taper ends. Place on a large greased cookie sheet sprinkled with cornmeal. Repeat to make 2 more loaves, placing them 2-inches apart on cookie sheet.
7 Cover; let rise in warm place, away from drafts, 30 minutes or until double in bulk. Make slits, 2-inches apart, on top of loaves with a very sharp knife or razor blade. Brush with egg white. Spray loaves with cold water (a well-washed window-spray cleaner bottle works perfectly or use a plant sprayer).
8 Place cookie sheet in lower third of preheated oven.
9 Bake in very hot oven (450°) 15 minutes. Reduce the heat to moderate (350°). Spray loaves again with water. Bake 30 minutes longer, or until bread gives a hollow sound when

tapped. Remove immediately from pan; cool. Serve same day or freeze until ready to use.

CRACKERS AND BREADS

It is best to choose mild-flavored bases for cheese tasting—more distinctively flavored crackers can overpower the taste of the cheese. It is generally best to avoid salted crackers for the same reason. Choose four from the assortment below.

Melba Toast Rounds	Soda Crackers
Sesame-seed Wafers	Rye Wafers
Unsalted Saltines	Water Crackers
Toast Triangles	Party-size Rye

Onion Mustard

Serve this French-style mustard with cold meat platters or on hearty meat sandwiches

Makes four 6-ounce jars.

2 large onions, chopped (2 cups)

2 cloves garlic, chopped
2 cups dry white wine
1 can (4 ounces) dry mustard
2 tablespoons honey
2 tablespoons vegetable oil
2 teaspoons salt
¼ teaspoon seasoned pepper

1 Combine onions, garlic and wine in a large saucepan; bring to boiling; lower heat; simmer 15 minutes; remove from heat; allow to stand 15 minutes.

2 Pour mixture, half at a time, into container of an electric blender; cover; process on high until smooth; pour into large bowl.

3 Combine dry mustard, honey and vegetable oil in same saucepan until smooth; blend in onion purée, salt and seasoned pepper.

4 Bring to boiling, stirring constantly; lower heat; cook, stirring constantly, 5 minutes, or until mixture thickens; pour into hot sterilized 6-ounce jars; seal, and process in hot-water bath 5 minutes.

GENERAL DIRECTIONS FOR CANNING AND WATER-BATH PROCESS

Follow directions carefully and do not take any shortcuts. Otherwise your rows of preserves will spoil in a few months.
1. Place hot-water-bath canner onto surface burner; add water to half-fill canner; cover canner; bring water to boiling while preparing jars and food.
2. Wash jars in hot sudsy water; rinse well; leave in hot water until ready to use.
3. Place new domed lids in a bowl and cover with boiling water; keep in water until ready to use.
4. Follow individual recipe directions.
5. Remove jars from water, individually; place on paper toweling or clean cloth; pack and/or ladle food into jars, leaving headroom called for in recipe.
6. Wipe top and outside rim of jar with clean cloth; place domed lid on top; screw metal rings on tightly, but do not use force.
7. Place jars in canner rack and lower into rapidly boiling water, adding additional boiling water to kettle if the level of the water is not 2-inches above the jars; cover kettle. Return to a full boil.
8. Process, following times given in individual recipes and calculated from time water comes to second boil.
Note: For those who live at altitudes above sea level, when recipe directions call for processing 20 minutes or less, add 1 minute for each 1,000 feet; when processing more than 20 minutes, add 2 minutes for each 1,000 feet.
9. Remove jars from canner and place on wire racks or cloth-lined surface at least 3-inches apart until cool, 12 hours.
10. Test all jars to be sure that they are sealed by tapping with a spoon. (A clear ringing sound means a good seal. If jars are not sealed properly, either store in refrigerator and plan to use within a month or pour contents of jar into a bowl and process again from Step 5.)
11. Remove metal rings; wipe jars with a clean dampened cloth; label, date and store jars in a cool, dark, dry place.

Madeira Cake

This cake is so rich you should serve it in very thin slices

Bake at 275° for 1½ hours.
Makes one large loaf.

1 jar (4 ounces) chopped candied citron
½ cup candied cherries, halved
½ cup golden raisins
¼ cup toasted slivered almonds
2¼ cups all-purpose flour
1 cup (2 sticks) butter or margarine
1 cup sugar
4 eggs
¼ cup Madeira or sherry

1 Line bottom and sides of a 9x5x3-inch loaf pan with a double thickness of brown paper; grease paper.
2 Combine citron, cherries, raisins and almonds in a medium-size bowl. Toss 1 cup of the flour with fruits.
3 Cream butter or margarine with sugar until fluffy in a large bowl with electric mixer at medium speed; beat in eggs, one at a time, then Madeira or sherry. Stir in remaining flour; fold in fruit mixture. Spoon into prepared pan.
4 Bake in very slow oven (275°) 1½ hours, or until a long thin skewer inserted in center comes out clean.
5 Cool 1 hour in pan on a wire rack; turn out; peel off paper; cool.
6 To store, slide cake into a plastic bag and seal. It will stay fresh and moist in the refrigerator for about 4 weeks, or in freezer for 3 months.

MAKE YOUR OWN BUFFET

Chicken and Chinese Cabbage Salad
Apricot-Wheat Germ-Corn Bread
Marinated Chick Peas, Tuna,
and Artichoke Hearts
Orange Whole-Wheat Bread
Garden Greens with Buttermilk Dressing
Shredded-Wheat Prune Bread
Spinach and Mushroom Salad
Banana-Honey-Bran Bread

Chicken and Chinese Cabbage Salad

Tasty variation of an old-time favorite

Makes 4 servings.

1 chicken breast (about 12 ounces)
1 package frozen snow peas
¼ cup peanut or vegetable oil
2 tablespoons cider vinegar
4½ teaspoons soy sauce
¾ teaspoon ground ginger
Pinch sugar and salt
¼ cup sliced green onion
1 cup bean sprouts
1 medium head Chinese cabbage
1 tablespoon toasted sesame seeds
½ cup coarsely chopped walnuts

1 Simmer chicken breast in salted water until tender, about 10 minutes. Skin, bone and cube (1½ cups).
2 Defrost snow peas; dry on paper towel.
3 Make dressing: Shake oil, vinegar, soy sauce, ginger, sugar and salt in a screw-top jar.
4 Toss chicken, snow peas, green onion and bean sprouts with the soy dressing; cover and refrigerate.
5 Slice enough cabbage to make 4 cups. Place in bowl; arrange chicken mixture on top. Sprinkle sesame seeds and walnuts over top. Toss lightly.

Apricot-Wheat Germ-Corn Bread

Quick bread that goes well with most buffets

Bake at 375° for 40 minutes.
Makes 2 small loaves.

⅔ cup sifted all-purpose flour
⅓ cup sugar
3½ teaspoons baking powder
1 teaspoon salt
⅔ cup wheat germ
⅔ cup yellow cornmeal
¾ cup yellow cornmeal
¾ cup chopped dried apricots
2 eggs
1 cup milk
¼ cup vegetable oil

1 Sift flour, sugar, baking powder and salt into a medium-size bowl. Stir in wheat germ, cornmeal and apricots.
2 Beat eggs slightly in a small bowl. Stir in milk and oil.

3 Pour liquid ingredients into dry and stir just until flour is evenly moist. Spoon batter into 2 greased 7⅞x3⅝x2¼-inch loaf pans
4 Bake in a moderate oven (375°) for 40 minutes or until wooden pick inserted in the centers comes out clean. Cool in pans on wire rack 10 minutes. Remove from pans; cool completely. Wrap in foil or plastic when cool; store overnight for easier slicing.

Marinated Chick Peas, Tuna and Artichoke Hearts

This salad stands alone at a buffet luncheon—as a side dish at a full buffet party

Makes 4 servings.

1 jar marinated artichoke hearts
1 can (20 ounces) chick peas, drained
1 can (7 ounces) tuna, drained and flaked
1 tablespoon lemon juice
½ teaspoon salt
¼ teaspoon ground cumin
¼ teaspoon cracked pepper
¼ cup chopped red onion
¼ cup chopped parsley
1 small head romaine lettuce
2 tomatoes, cut into wedges
   Ripe olives (optional)

1 Drain artichoke hearts, reserving oil. Halve and place in medium-size bowl with chick peas and tuna.
2 Combine lemon juice, salt, cumin and pepper with reserved oil; pour over chick pea-tuna-artichoke mixture; stir in onion and parsley; cover and refrigerate several hours.
3 Wash romaine; dry well; break into pieces and place in salad bowl; cover and refrigerate until serving time.
4 When ready to serve, add chick pea mixture to romaine. Toss lightly to coat with dressing. Arrange tomato wedges and olives around edges.

Orange Whole-Wheat Bread

There is plenty of nutrition in this exotic bread

Bake at 350° for 1 hour.
Makes 1 large loaf.

2 cups sifted all-purpose flour
1 cup sugar

3½ teaspoons baking powder
1 teaspoon salt
1 cup whole wheat flour
¾ cup crunchy nut-like cereal nuggets
1 egg
4 teaspoons grated orange rind
¾ cup orange juice
¾ cup milk
¼ cup (½ stick) butter or margarine, melted

1 Sift all-purpose flour, sugar, baking powder and salt into a large bowl. Stir in whole wheat flour and cereal nuggets.
2 Beat egg slightly in small bowl. Stir in orange rind and juice, milk and butter.
3 Pour liquid ingredients into dry and stir just until flour is evenly moist. Spoon batter into greased 9x5x3-inch loaf pan.
4 Bake in a moderate oven (350°) for 1 hour or until a wooden pick inserted in the center comes out clean. Cool in pan on wire rack 10 minutes. Remove from pan; cool completely. Wrap in foil or plastic when cool; store overnight.

Garden Greens with Buttermilk Dressing

The piquant dressing has only 12 calories per serving

Makes 4 servings.

½ cup buttermilk
½ clove garlic, mashed
¼ teaspoon sugar
¼ teaspoon dry mustard
¼ teaspoon salt
⅛ teaspoon pepper
1 quart salad greens (chicory, romaine, watercress and Boston lettuce)
1 cucumber, pared and sliced
4 radishes, sliced
4 ounces Swiss cheese, cut into matchstick pieces

1 For Dressing: Combine buttermilk, garlic, sugar, mustard, salt and pepper in measuring cup. Stir to mix well
2 Wash, dry and tear the salad greens into pieces. Place in salad bowl with cucumber, radishes and cheese.
3 Pour dressing over; toss to coat.

Shredded-Wheat Prune Bread

A wholesome spicy dark bread

Bake at 350° for 1 hour.
Makes 1 loaf.

1¾ cups sifted all-purpose flour
2 teaspoons baking powder
1 teaspoon ground cinnamon
½ teaspoon salt
⅓ cup butter or margarine
⅔ cup sugar
2 eggs
1 teaspoon grated lemon rind
½ cup milk
1 cup crumbled shredded wheat
1 cup chopped pitted prunes

1 Sift flour, baking powder, cinnamon and salt onto wax paper.
2 Beat butter or margarine, sugar and eggs in a large bowl with electric mixer at high speed until light and fluffy. Stir in lemon rind.
3 Stir in flour mixture alternately with milk until batter is smooth. Stir in shredded wheat and prunes. Spoon into greased 8½x4½x2½-inch loaf pan.
4 Bake in a moderate oven (350°) for 1 hour or until a wooden pick inserted in the center comes out clean. Cool in pan on wire rack 10 minutes. Remove from pan; cool completely. Wrap in foil or plastic when cool; store overnight.

Spinach and Mushroom Salad

Fresh spinach with a tangy dressing

Makes 4 servings.

4 slices bacon
2 teaspoons sugar
2 tablespoons cider vinegar
2 tablespoons water
½ teaspoon salt
1 pound fresh loose spinach
¼ pound fresh mushrooms, sliced
2 medium-size carrots, pared and shredded
2 hard-cooked eggs, cut into wedges

1 Cook bacon in skillet; remove to paper toweling; crumble and reserve. Measure bacon fat; return 2 tablespoons to skillet. Stir in sugar, vinegar, water and salt. Keep warm over low heat.

2 Wash and remove stems from spinach; dry thoroughly and break into pieces in salad bowl. Pour warm dressing over and toss until coated and wilted.
3 Top with mushrooms, carrots and bacon; toss. Garnish with eggs.

Banana-Honey-Bran Bread

A nice moist bread that keeps well

Bake at 350° for 1 hour.
Makes 1 loaf.

1½ cups sifted all-purpose flour
2 teaspoons baking powder
½ teaspoon baking soda
½ teaspoon salt
1 cup whole bran cereal
¼ cup chopped walnuts
1 egg
½ cup honey
¼ cup vegetable oil
¼ cup milk
1½ cups mashed ripe bananas

1 Sift flour, baking powder, baking soda and salt into a large bowl. Stir in cereal and nuts.
2 Beat egg slightly in a small bowl, then beat in honey, oil, milk and banana.
3 Add banana mixture all at once to dry ingredients and stir just until flour is dampened. Spoon batter into a greased 9x5x3-inch loaf pan.
4 Bake in a moderate oven (350°) for 1 hour or until a wooden pick inserted in center comes out clean. Cool in pan on wire rack 10 minutes. Remove from pan; cool completely. Wrap in foil or plastic; when cool, store overnight.

MAKE YOUR OWN BUFFET FOR TEENAGERS

Cranberry Fizz
Creamy Shrimp Dip Tray
Rolled Roast Beef
Stuffed Baked Potatoes
Tomato-Lima Cups
Parker House Cheesies
Candy Blossom Cake
Coffee　　　Milk

THE SHOPPING LIST

Roast beef (one 4 to 5-pound rolled boned rib roast)
Shrimps (one 5-ounce can)
Dairy sour cream (one 8-ounce carton)
Sliced American cheese (one 8-ounce package)
Baking potatoes (6 large)
Fresh tomatoes (6 medium)
Water cress (1 bunch)
Lettuce (1 head)
Parsley (1 bunch)
Frozen baby lima beans (one 10-ounce package)
Ready-baked Parker House rolls (1 dozen)
Corn chips (1 package, to go with dip)
Favorite crackers (1 box), to go with dip
Yellow cake mix (1 package)
Fluffy white frosting mix (2 packages)
Cranberry-juice cocktail (one 16-ounce bottle)
Imitation citrus-flavor carbonated beverage (one 10-ounce bottle)
Green-onion dip mix (1 envelope)
Flavored marshmallows, tiny gumdrops, and leaf-shape jelly candies (enough to decorate cake)

TAKE FROM THE REFRIGERATOR OR CUPBOARD

Mayonnaise or salad dressing
Butter or margarine
Milk
Eggs
Catsup
Horseradish
Lemons
Salt and pepper
Vegetable oil
Vinegar
Sugar
Paprika
Almond extract
Yellow food coloring
Maraschino cherries
Toasted slivered almonds
Stuffed green olives
Pitted ripe olives
Pimiento

SUGGESTED WORK PLAN

The day before:
1 Put bottles of cranberry juice and carbonated beverage in refrigerator.
2 Mix shrimp dip; cover dish; chill.
3 Peel tomatoes; place on a plate, cover and chill.
4 Cook lima beans; toss with dressing; cover dish and chill.

5 Bake cake layers; cool and wrap. Chop maraschino cherries for filling; set aside in covered dish. Make marshmallow flowers; wrap in transparent wrap so they won't dry out. All of these foods can be left on counter top or go on a shelf, as Mother prefers.
6 Scrub and dry potatoes; leave on counter top. Wash lettuce and water cress; dry well on paper toweling; place in vegetable crisper in refrigerator.

The morning of the dinner:
1 Make cake filling and frosting; put layers together and decorate completely.
2 Get cheese rolls ready for baking; place on cookie sheet. Wrap in transparent wrap and set aside until time to heat (10 minutes before serving time).
3 Make olive-pimiento decorations for tomato salads and cut lemon slices for punch. Wrap separately (plastic bags are good) and put in refrigerator.

Starting about 3 hours before dinner:
1 Season roast and put in oven.
2 When meat has been in about an hour, place potatoes in with it.
3 Set the table.
4 Scoop out insides of tomatoes and fill with lima beans; lay lettuce leaves on salad plates and top each with a tomato cup. Refrigerate until serving time.
5 Make coffee.
6 Take potatoes out of oven when done; scoop and refill them; put back in oven to reheat.
7 Spoon shrimp dip into serving bowl; arrange on tray with corn chips and crackers.
8 Remove roast from oven and place on serving platter; cover with foil and let stand (makes slicing easier).
9 Mix cranberry punch; take pitcher, glasses, and shrimp tray into living room to serve.
10 Place rolls in oven to heat.
11 Remove potatoes and rolls from oven; place on serving plates.
12 Garnish salads; place on table; bring roast beef to table.
13 Clear table; serve cake and coffee.

Cranberry Fizz

Light and with a sparkling taste

Makes 6 servings.

1 bottle (16 ounces) cranberry-juice cocktail, chilled

(continued)

1 bottle (10 ounces) low-calorie imitation cit-
rus-flavor carbonated beverage, chilled
1 lemon, cut in 6 slices

1 Just before serving, mix cranberry-juice cocktail and carbonated beverage in a large pitcher; pour into 6 small glasses.

2 Make a slit in each lemon slice from outside edge to center; hang over edge of each glass. (To make notched slices as pictured, cut small V-shape pieces all the way around from rind of each slice with a small sharp-tip knife.)

Rolled Roast Beef

Let Mother supervise the cooking of this expensive roast

Roast at 325° for 2 to 2½ hours.
Makes 6 servings plus enough for one bonus meal.

1 rolled boned rib roast of beef, weighing 4 to
5 pounds
2 teaspoons salt
Watercress

1 Preheat oven to slow (325°).
2 Wipe roast with damp paper toweling. Sprinkle meat all over with salt, then place, fat side up, on a rack in an open roasting pan. Stick meat thermometer into roast so the bulb end reaches the center of the meat. Do not add water or cover pan. Place in oven.
3 Roast in slow oven (325°) 2 to 2½ hours, or until thermometer registers 140° for rare or 160° for medium.
4 Remove meat from oven and place on a serving platter; cover loosely with foil and let stand about 20 minutes. (This makes roast easier to slice.)
5 Cut 2 or 3 strings away from meat, then trim

a thin slice from the bottom so roast will stand upright on platter. Place sprigs of watercress around meat.

Creamy Shrimp Dip Tray

Serve this to the adults in the living room

Makes 6 servings.

1 can (about 5 ounces) deveined shrimps
½ cup mayonnaise or salad dressing
½ cup dairy sour cream
¼ cup catsup
1 teaspoon lemon juice
1 teaspoon prepared horseradish
  Corn chips
  Crackers

1 Empty shrimps into a sieve and rinse under cold water. Set aside 1 shrimp for garnish; cut remainder into small pieces.
2 Combine mayonnaise or salad dressing, sour cream, catsup, lemon juice, and horseradish in a medium-size bowl; fold in shrimps. Chill at least two hours or overnight to blend flavors.
3 Spoon into a small bowl. Garnish with saved shrimp and a tiny sprig of parsley, if you wish. Serve with corn chips and crisp crackers.

Stuffed Baked Potatoes

Make sure the potatoes are large and firm

Bake at 325° for 1¾ hours.
Makes 6 servings.

6 large baking potatoes
  Vegetable oil

¾ cup milk
4 tablespoons (½ stick) butter or margarine
1 envelope (2 packets) green-onion dip mix

1 Scrub potatoes with a vegetable brush; dry with paper toweling. Rub skins all over with vegetable oil to keep them soft. Place potatoes in a large shallow pan.

2 Bake in same slow oven (325°) with roast, 1½ hours, or until potatoes are soft; remove from oven but leave heat turned on.
3 Using pot holders to protect your fingers, cut a slice lengthwise from top of each potato and lift off. Carefully scoop out the insides with a teaspoon and place in a large bowl. (Be careful not to break shells.) Return shells to pan.
4 Combine milk, butter or margarine, and onion-dip mix in a small saucepan; heat slowly until butter melts.
5 Mash potatoes in bowl; beat in hot milk mixture until potatoes are fluffy. Spoon back into shells, mounding slightly. Return to oven.
6 Bake 15 minutes longer, or until lightly browned on top. Arrange potatoes on a serving platter. If you wish, sprinkle potatoes with sliced fresh green onions, pressing slices down lightly into potatoes, and use the green tops to trim the platter.

Tomato-Lima Cups

Here's a chance for the teenager to show off her—or his—creative talents

Makes 6 servings.

1 package (10 ounces) frozen baby lima beans
¾ teaspoon salt

(continued)

½ teaspoon sugar
¼ teaspoon paprika
⅛ teaspoon pepper
½ cup chopped parsley
⅓ cup vegetable oil
3 tablespoons cider vinegar
6 medium-size firm ripe tomatoes. washed
   Lettuce
6 stuffed green olives
3 small pitted ripe olives, halved crosswise
1 pimiento, cut in 6 strips

1 Cook lima beans, following label directions; drain well; place in a medium-size bowl.
2 Measure salt, sugar, paprika, pepper, parsley, vegetable oil, and vinegar into beans; toss until well-mixed and beans are shiny. Cover with transparent wrap and chill several hours or overnight.
3 Heat a pan of water just until bubbly. Holding tomatoes, one at a time, on a slotted spoon, dip into water and hold about a minute, then lift out and place in a pie plate to cool. Cut a thin slice from the top of each tomato, then peel off skin. Scoop out the insides with a teaspoon, being careful not to break shells. Turn tomatoes upside down in plate to drain; cover and chill.
4 One or two hours before serving, place a large lettuce leaf on each of 6 salad plates; stand a tomato cup on each leaf; spoon lima bean mixture into cups.
5 Slide a green olive onto each of 6 wooden picks, then a piece of ripe olive and a strip of pimiento. Stand one pick in center of each tomato cup. Chill until serving time.

Parker House Cheesies

To the teenage cook: Don't let your Mother see you cook these—watch her expression as you place them on the table

Bake at 325° for 10 minutes.
Makes 6 servings.

12 ready-baked Parker House rolls
3 slices process American cheese (from an
   8-ounce package)

1 Separate rolls, then pull each apart slightly at the fold.
2 Cut each slice of cheese in half lengthwise, then in half crosswise; cut each piece into 2 small triangles. Tuck 2 triangles, one on top of

the other, in each roll; press edges together. Place rolls on a cookie sheet.
3 Heat in slow oven (325°) 10 minutes, or until cheese starts to melt.

Candy Blossom Cake

This is the final dish that will have the adults talking about your culinary skills for months—keep a camera on hand

Bake at 350° for 30 minutes.
Makes 1 nine-inch layer cake.

1 package yellow cake mix
   Eggs
   Water
2 packages fluffy white frosting mix
   Boiling water

(continued)

A cheese and fruit bowl is the perfect accompaniment to the buffet made by a teenager.

⅓ cup toasted slivered almonds (from a 5-ounce can)
⅓ cup chopped maraschino cherries
½ teaspoon almond extract
Yellow food coloring
10 flavored marshmallows (from a 10-ounce package)
Tiny colored gumdrops and leaf-shape jelly candies

1 Preheat oven to moderate (350°).
2 Grease bottoms of 2 nine-inch layer-cake pans; line with wax paper; grease paper.
3 Prepare cake mix with eggs and water, following label directions; pour into prepared cake pans, dividing evenly.
4 Bake in moderate oven (350°) 30 minutes, or until tops spring back when lightly pressed with fingertip. Cool in pans on wire racks 5 minutes. Run the tip of a small knife around inside edges of pans to loosen layers; invert onto racks; peel off wax paper; cool layers completely.
5 Prepare both packages of frosting mix with boiling water, following label directions. Measure 1 cup of the frosting into another small bowl and stir in almonds, cherries, and almond extract. Set aside. (This will be cake filling.)
6 Stir a few drops yellow food coloring into remaining frosting to tint pale yellow.
7 Brush around edges of cake layers with a pastry brush to remove any loose crumbs. Place one layer, top side down, on a serving plate. Spread with almond-cherry filling, spreading not quite to edge; place second layer, flat side down, on top. Spread yellow frosting around side and top of cake, piling any extra frosting in center of top to hold candy flowers.
8 To make flowers, cut each marshmallow in

half crosswise with scissors. (To keep scissors from sticking, dip blades in 10X [confectioners' powdered] sugar, tapping off any extra.) Holding each piece of marshmallow, flat side down, snip 6 times around edge, cutting from outside almost to center.
9 Cut tops off 20 gumdrops with a small knife; place one in the center of each marshmallow flower. Arrange on top of cake. Place leaf-shape candies around flowers.

STEP-BY-STEP HOW-TO

To help teenagers off to a good start, suggest a look at the pictures on the pages in this section. Color photos show the finished foods; the others, how special steps are done.
Cranberry Fizz, *for example, is trimmed with fancy-edge lemon slices. Our young cook is shown making these at the top of the page by cutting out tiny V-shape pieces all around the edge of each slice.*
Creamy Shrimp Dip, *served with the punch and next to it in the color photo, is so easy that no how-to photo is needed.*
Rolled Roast Beef and Stuffed Baked Potatoes *are served together, so that's how we'll talk about them. After potatoes are baked, the insides are scooped out, mashed, and put back in the shells. Our cook shows how to handle a hot potato—with a pot holder for protection. The big beautiful roast is actually simplest of all—just leave it in the oven till it's done. Best way to be sure: Use a meat thermometer. Push it, bulb end down, through top of roast into center.*
Tomato-Lima Cup *salad calls for peeled tomatoes—a cinch when you dip each one in a pan of hot water, hold it there about a minute. Skin will peel right off.*
Parker House Cheesies *are another snap: Ready-baked rolls with cheese triangles tucked in folds, heated for 10 minutes.*
Candy Blossom Cake *sprouts marshmallow flowers. To make, cut marshmallows in half, snip around edge of each half with scissors, put piece of gumdrop in center. For a neat, pretty frosting job, do the side first, moving spatula up and down instead of sideways, then frost top.*

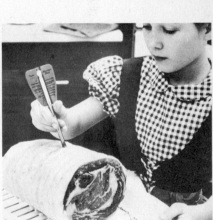

Buffets For The Season

"April comes but once a year," and so does New Year's, Easter, May Day, July 4th, Thanksgiving, and Christmas. Each year these events present a party problem. The following buffets take the worry out of that problem.

NEW YEAR'S BUFFET

Holiday Punch Bowl
Sausage Tartlets
Tomatoes Pyrenees
Seafood Newburg
Curried Chicken and Vegetables
Fluffy Rice
Ribbon Salad Bowl
Hot Rolls
Christmas Ice Cream Log
Coffee Tea

Holiday Punch Bowl

Watch the excitement when your guests see the "Orange Volcanoes" that fume and bubble around the ruby punch

Makes 20 punch-cup servings

6 envelopes (⅝-ounce each) instant daiquiri mix
2 cups light rum
1 can (46 ounces) fruit juicy red Hawaiian punch, chilled
1 bottle (28 ounces) quinine water
ICE MOLD (recipe follows)
1 orange, cut in thin slices
ORANGE VOLCANOES (recipe follows)

1 Dissolve daiquiri mix in rum in a medium-size bowl; refrigerate.
2 Party time: Pour rum mixture into punch bowl; add punch and quinine water; carefully slide in ICE MOLD and add orange slices. Place ORANGE VOLCANOES around punch-bowl tray. Decorate with Christmas greens, if you wish.

Take care of the New Year good-intention blues with this fabulous buffet: **Seafood Newburg, Ribbon Salad Bowl,** and **Christmas Ice-Cream Log.**

ICE MOLD

Fill an 8-cup mold with water; set in freezer for four hours, or overnight. To unmold, let stand at room temperature about 5 minutes, or until ice is movable in mold. Invert onto a cookie sheet and slide carefully into filled punch bowl.

ORANGE VOLCANOES

Cut a slice from the top of each of 4 large oranges; hollow out, saving fruit for a family treat. Cut tops of oranges in sawtooth design. (This can be done the day before and the oranges wrapped in plastic bags and refrigerated.) Party time: Fill orange shells to within ½ inch of top with water. Place several small pieces of dry ice (handle with care and use tongs) in each orange shell. As smoke dies down, add several more small pieces of dry ice. **Note:** Dry ice from your local ice company.

Sausage Tartlets

Tiny tarts with a savory filling

Bake shells at 400° for 5 minutes, then at 375° for 15 minutes. Heat at 400° for 10 minutes.
Makes about 5 dozen

1 package piecrust mix
5 brown 'n serve sausages (½ an 8-ounce package)
¼ pound mushrooms, finely chopped
1 small onion, chopped (¼ cup)
1 egg
½ cup milk
½ cup shredded Cheddar cheese
½ teaspoon salt
½ teaspoon leaf marjoram, crumbled
¼ teaspoon pepper

1 Prepare piecrust mix, following label directions. Pinch off small pieces; press into 1¼-inch tartlet pans. If tartlet pans are not available, tiny muffin pans may be used, pressing the piecrust mix about half way up the sides of the cups. Place tartlet pans in a baking pan for ease in handling.
2 Bake in hot oven (400°) 5 minutes. Remove to wire rack.
3 Cut sausages into very thin slices. Brown in a small skillet; remove to paper toweling with a slotted spoon. Sauté mushrooms and onion in pan drippings until just tender.

(continued)

4 Beat egg slightly in a medium-size bowl; add milk, cheese, salt, marjoram and pepper. Mix well. Fill tartlet shells, dividing sausage slices evenly.
5 Bake in moderate oven (375°) 15 minutes, or until firm. Remove to wire rack. Let stand a few minutes before removing tartlets from pans.
6 Do-ahead note: Place tartlets in foil or plastic boxes; cover firmly: label and freeze.
7 Party day: Place tartlets in baking pan. Heat in hot oven (400°) about 10 minutes, or until piping-hot. Garnish each with a thin slice of stuffed olive, if you wish. Keep hot on hot tray.

Tomatoes Pyrenees

Cherry tomatoes are tossed in garlic-flavored oil and chopped parsley for a quick and colorful treat

Makes about 4 dozen

1 pint cherry tomatoes
3 tablespoons olive or vegetable oil
1 clove of garlic, minced
¼ cup finely chopped parsley

1 Stem and wash tomatoes; dry on paper toweling.
2 Heat oil with garlic in a skillet. Add tomatoes and parsley; toss gently to coat and heat tomatoes but not to burst skins.
3 Do-ahead note: This may be done early in the day. Cover tomatoes and chill until serving time.
4 Party time: Insert a food pick into each tomato and place on a hot tray, or return to skillet and heat for several minutes.

Seafood Newburg

Succulent seafood, swimming in sherried cream sauce, adds a touch of elegance to any dinner party

Makes 8 servings

1 lobster (about 1 pound)
OR: 2 packages (7 ounces each) frozen Rock lobster tails, cooked
6 tablespoons (¾ stick) butter or margarine
⅓ cup flour
1½ teaspoons salt
¼ teaspoon cayenne
¼ teaspoon ground nutmeg

1 cup milk
1 cup cream for whipping
3 egg yolks
½ cup dry sherry
1 pound scallops, cooked
1 pound shrimp, cleaned, deveined and cooked
6 cups hot cooked rice

1 Remove meat from lobster or lobster tails, saving shell or tail shells for garnishing platter, if you wish. Cut meat into bite-size pieces; reserve.
2 Melt butter or margarine in a large saucepan; stir in flour, salt, cayenne and nutmeg; cook, stirring constantly, until bubbly. Stir in milk and cream; continue cooking and stirring until sauce thickens and bubbles 1 minute; remove from heat.
3 Beat egg yolks slightly in a small bowl; stir in sherry. Slowly stir in a generous ½ cup of the hot sauce, then stir back into remaining sauce in pan. Cook slowly, stirring constantly, 1 minute. Fold in scallops, shrimp and lobster. Heat gently about 5 minutes.
4 Do-ahead note: Line top of an 8-cup double boiler with heavy foil. Spoon in seafood mixture; freeze. When frozen, remove foil-wrapped food from double boiler; return to freezer.
5 Party day: Remove foil from frozen seafood mixture and place in top of double boiler; cover. Heat over hot water 1½ to 2 hours, until thawed and bubbly-hot. Serve over hot rice. Garnish platter with reserved shells and parsley sprigs, if you wish.

Curried Chicken and Vegetables

A different curry—tender boneless chicken breasts in an aromatic curried vegetable sauce, served over steaming rice

Makes 8 servings

4 whole chicken breasts, split (about 12 ounces each)
¼ cup flour (for chicken)
½ teaspoon salt (for chicken)
⅛ teaspoon pepper (for chicken)
¼ cup (½ stick) butter or margarine
1 large onion, chopped (1 cup)
1 green pepper, halved, seeded and diced
1 tablespoon flour (for sauce)
1 teaspoon salt (for sauce)
⅛ teaspoon pepper (for sauce)
2 tablespoons curry powder
1 can (8 ounces) tomatoes

2 envelopes or teaspoons instant chicken broth
2¼ cups water
6 cups hot cooked rice

1 Pull skin from split chicken breasts; bone. Flatten each half by placing between two pieces of wax paper and pounding with the back of a heavy knife or mallet. Cut each half into 2 pieces (fillets).
2 Combine ¼ cup flour, ½ teaspoon salt and ⅛ teaspoon pepper in a plastic bag. Add chicken fillets; shake well to coat.
3 Melt butter or margarine in a large skillet; sauté chicken fillets until brown on both sides. Remove from skillet.
4 Sauté onion and green pepper until almost tender in same skillet. Stir in the 1 tablespoon flour, 1 teaspoon salt, ⅛ teaspoon pepper and curry powder. Add tomatoes, instant chicken broth and water; bring to boiling.
5 Lower heat; simmer, covered, 20 minutes. Remove cover and simmer 5 minutes longer, or until sauce thickens.
6 Return chicken fillets to sauce and cover. Simmer 15 minutes longer, or until chicken is tender.
7 Do-ahead note: Line a 10-cup shallow freezer-to-table baking dish with heavy foil. Arrange chicken in dish and spoon sauce over; wrap; label and freeze. When frozen, remove foil-wrapped food from dish; return to freezer.
8 Party day: Remove food from freezer and peel off foil. Place in same dish. Bake, covered, in moderate oven (350°) 1 hour, or until bubbly-hot. Serve with hot rice.

Ribbon Salad Bowl

This colorful vegetable salad, with its finely chopped greens, is dressed and served (no tossing needed) a section at a time, so it stays crisp and lively to the party's end

Makes 8 servings

1 package (10 ounces) frozen Fordhook lima beans
1 package (10 ounces) frozen cut wax beans
1 envelope Italian salad-dressing mix
1 envelope bleu cheese salad-dressing mix
1⅓ cups vegetable oil
½ cup vinegar
¼ cup water
1 small head romaine, finely chopped
1 small head iceberg, finely chopped
1 package (10 ounces) fresh spinach, finely chopped

2 bunches radishes, thinly sliced
2 cucumbers, scored and thinly sliced

1 Cook lima beans and wax beans in separate small saucepans, following label directions. Drain and place in a shallow dish in separate mounds.
2 Prepare Italian and bleu cheese salad-dressing mixes together with oil, vinegar and water in a large jar with a screw top. Pour about ½ cup of dressing over hot vegetables.
3 Do-ahead note: Cover and chill vegetables. (You can also prepare greens, radishes and cucumbers and wrap in plastic and chill.)
4 Party time: Layer romaine, iceberg and spinach in a large salad bowl. Arrange radishes, lima beans, cucumber slices and wax beans in rows on top of greens. Pour remaining dressing over salad, just before serving.

Christmas Ice Cream Log

This little beauty doesn't need a special mold. A clean empty juice can will do just fine

Makes 8 to 10 servings

½ cup chopped maraschino cherries
½ cup maraschino cherry juice
Few drops red food coloring
1 quart vanilla ice cream
⅓ cup creme de menthe
1½ pints lemon sherbet, slightly softened
1 cup cream for whipping
3 whole red maraschino cherries with stems
4 whole candied green cherries

1 Stir chopped cherries, cherry juice and red food coloring quickly into vanilla ice cream in a medium-size bowl. Using back of spoon or rubber scraper, press ice cream evenly around inside of a 46-ounce juice can (about ¾ inch thick). Freeze at least 2 hours, or until firm.
2 Stir crème de menthe quickly into lemon sherbet in a medium-size bowl; spoon into center of can; cover with foil or transparent wrap. Freeze, in an upright position, at least 6 hours, or overnight.
3 Unmold one or two hours before serving. To unmold: Loosen around edge of mold with a sharp knife; dip mold, in an upright position, quickly into a large saucepan of hot water. Invert onto a plate; shake to loosen; remove mold. Turn the log on side. Cover; return to freezer until surface is firm.
4 When ready to serve, beat the cream until stiff in a medium-size bowl. Remove stems from

(continued)

whole cherries; reserve. With a small sharp knife, cut maraschino cherries ¾ of the way down into 6 sections each, to make petals. Cut candied green cherries in half and place one half into the center of each of the 3 cherry flowers. Cut green leaves from the green candied cherries and reserve.

5 Attach a rosette tip to a pastry bag; spoon whipped cream into bag. Press out into rosettes along bottom and sides and top of ice cream log. Garnish with cherry flowers, leaves and stems. To serve, cut into slices.

FESTIVE EASTER BUFFET

Eggs with Pink Mayonnaise*
Baked Lemon-Ginger Ham*
Buttered Whole Green Beans
or
Asparagus a la Francaise*
Baby Carrots
Buttered Potatoes with Chives
Cucumber and Spinach Salad
Braided Poppy Seed Rolls
Rhubarb Raspberry Soufflé*

Eggs with Pink Mayonnaise

An attractive first course and a wonderful way to use leftover hard-cooked Easter eggs

Makes 8 servings.

½ package unflavored gelatin
¼ cup water
½ cup mayonnaise or salad dressing
2 tablespoons chili sauce
½ teaspoon salt
4 drops liquid hot pepper seasoning
8 hard-cooked eggs, shelled
Celery leaves and stems
Mayonnaise
Hard-cooked egg yolk
Watercress

1 Sprinkle gelatin over water in small saucepan. Dissolve over *very low* heat.
2 Mix ½ cup mayonnaise or salad dressing, chili sauce, salt and hot pepper seasoning in small bowl until smooth. Gradually stir in half the dissolved gelatin.
3 Dip eggs, one at a time, in mixture to coat evenly. Arrange in a baking pan; refrigerate just until set. Keep remaining gelatin at room tem-

perature. Cut celery leaves into blade-like leaf shapes, ¼x1-inch in size. Cut stems into thin ⅛-inch slivers about 1 inch long. Dip in gelatin remaining in pan. (Reheat if it has solidified.)
4 For decoration: Arrange leaves and a stem on each egg. Make a small paper cone with wax paper; fill with spoonful of mayonnaise. Cut tip to ⅛-inch opening. Pipe a daisy on each egg at tip of stem. Sprinkle center of daisy with mashed yolk.
5 Cover top of pan with plastic wrap so that it does not touch eggs. Chill until ready to serve, up to 2 hours. Transfer eggs with broad spatula to watercress-lined plate.

Baked Lemon-Ginger Ham

A ham with a difference! It has pockets of lemon rind, ginger and pineapple, and it's glazed and decorated with lemon slices

Bake at 325° for about 3 hours.
Makes 8 servings plus leftovers.

1 can (8¼ ounces) sliced pineapple in pineapple juice
1 jar (10 ounces) ginger preserved in syrup
4 lemons
1 bone-in fully cooked ham, about 12 pounds
1 tablespoon cornstarch

1 Drain pineapple, reserving juice in saucepan. Cut slices into ½-inch pieces. Drain syrup from ginger into saucepan with pineapple juice. Shred enough ginger to measure ¼ cup.
2 Grate rind of two lemons and remove rind of other two with a vegetable parer. Combine pineapple pieces, shredded ginger and grated lemon rind in small bowl.
3 Trim any skin and excess fat from ham to leave a ¼-inch fat layer. Make deep cuts with a small paring knife about 1 inch apart in fat side of ham. Widen cuts with finger or use handle of wooden spoon; press a flavored pineapple piece into each cut. Place ham, fat side up, in shallow roasting pan.
4 Bake in slow oven (325°) for 15 minutes a pound, or about 3 hours. About 30 minutes before ham is done, blend cornstarch into reserved juice and syrup. Cook until thickened, stirring constantly. Brush some over ham; bake 20 minutes more. Transfer to platter.
5 While ham rests 20 minutes, prepare garnish. Cut strips of lemon rind into julienne strips; boil in water several minutes; drain. Cut off all white membrane from lemons; slice. Garnish ham with

(continued)

This **Festive Easter Buffet** means **Baked Lemon-Ginger Ham** with **Buttered Whole Green Beans,** baby carrots.

sliced lemons and halved ginger, holding slices in place with halved wooden picks if needed. Dip julienned rind in leftover glaze; sprinkle on top of ham. Tuck parsley here and there, if you wish. Surround ham with vegetables.

Asparagus a la Francaise

Tender green spears over a bed of shredded lettuce

Makes 8 servings.

3 pounds fresh asparagus
3 tablespoons butter or margarine
4 cups shredded lettuce
6 sprigs parsley
1 tablespoon sugar
1½ teaspoons salt
3 tiny white onions, sliced and separated into rings
1 teaspoon flour
1 tablespoon butter or margarine, softened

1 Pare asparagus stalks thinly with a vegetable parer. Wash stalks well. Break off tough ends. Cut spears into 3- or 4-inch lengths.
2 Melt 3 tablespoons butter or margarine in large skillet. Add lettuce, parsley, sugar and salt. Arrange asparagus on top, keeping stalks parallel to each other. Top with onion rings. Bring to boiling; lower heat; cover. Simmer 10 minutes or until asparagus is just tender. Discard parsley.
3 Blend flour and butter to a paste; add to liquid in bottom of pan. Cook until sauce is thickened, stirring carefully so that asparagus is not tossed. Lift lettuce, then asparagus and onion rings with tongs to platter surrounding ham or serve in separate dish. Spoon pan juices on top.

Rhubarb and Raspberry Soufflé

A refreshing light dessert for a spring dinner: there's no last-minute fuss because it's made ahead

Makes 8 to 10 servings.

4 cups frozen unsweetened cut rhubarb (about 1 pound package), or fresh rhubarb, if available
¾ cup sugar
2 tablespoons cornstarch

Dash salt
1 cup water
⅓ cup orange liqueur or juice
1 tablespoon lemon juice
2 envelopes unflavored gelatin
½ cup cold water
1 package (10 ounces) frozen raspberries
4 large egg whites, at room temperature
½ cup sugar
1 cup heavy cream

1 Mix rhubarb, ¾ cup sugar, cornstarch and salt in a large saucepan; stir in 1 cup water. Cook mixture until rhubarb is tender, stirring often. Stir in orange liqueur and lemon juice; cook 1 minute more.
2 Remove 2 cups rhubarb mixture for sauce; chill. Sprinkle gelatin over the ½ cup water; let stand a minute to soften. Stir into rhubarb remaining in pan; stir in raspberries. Cook mixture over low heat just until gelatin is dissolved and raspberries are thawed. Pour mixture into container of electric blender. Cover; whirl until smooth. Strain to remove seeds. Cool slightly.
3 Beat egg whites until foamy in large bowl with electric mixer. Beat in the ½ cup sugar, 1 tablespoon at a time, until soft peaks form. Fold rhubarb mixture gently into whites.
4 Wash and dry beaters. Whip cream in a small bowl until stiff. Fold into rhubarb mixture. Pour into a glass bowl or an 8-cup soufflé dish with a 2-inch foil collar. Chill until firm. Spoon rhubarb sauce on top or serve in bowl along with the soufflé.

JULY 4th PICNIC BUFFET

Stuffed Chicken Napoli
Chili Spoonburgers
Garden Potato Salad
Calico Vegetable Crunch
Your Favorite Green Salad
French Bread
Sugar Crunch Squares
Brown-Eyed Susans
Fresh Fruit Basket
Pitcher Punch

Stuffed Chicken Napoli

Each crackly golden piece hides a zippy salami stuffing for a different flavor

Makes 8 servings

8 chicken drumsticks with thighs (about 5 pounds)

1 piece (4 ounces) salami
½ cup sifted all-purpose flour
2 teaspoons salt
1 teaspoon paprika
1 teaspoon leaf oregano, crumbled
⅛ teaspoon pepper
½ cup vegetable oil

1 Cut through chicken legs at joints to separate drum sticks and thighs, then cut an opening along bone of each drumstick and in meaty part of each thigh with a sharp knife to make a pocket for stuffing.
2 Cut salami into 16 strips; stuff 1 strip into each piece of chicken.
3 Shake pieces, a few at a time, in mixture of flour, salt, paprika, oregano and pepper in a paper bag to coat evenly.
4 Cook pieces slowly in vegetable oil in a large frying pan 20 minutes; turn; cover loosely. Cook 20 minutes longer, or until tender and crisply golden. Serve warm or cold.
Note—Pack pieces in a large shallow pan lined with paper toweling. Cover tightly.

Chili Spoonburgers

Hot and spicy—just right for any July 4th

Makes 8 servings.

2 pounds ground beef
1 large onion, chopped (1 cup)
1 cup thinly sliced celery
1 can (about 1 pound) stewed tomatoes
1 can (12 or 16 ounces) whole-kernel corn
1 can (4½ ounces) chopped ripe olives
¾ cup bottled chili sauce
2 teaspoons salt
2 teaspoons garlic salt
¼ teaspoon pepper
1 bay leaf
16 split hamburger buns, buttered

1 Shape ground beef into a large patty in a kettle or Dutch oven. Brown 5 minutes on each side, then break up into chunks. Stir in onion and celery; cook, stirring several times, 5 minutes longer.
2 Stir in tomatoes, corn and liquid, olives, chili sauce, salt, garlic salt, pepper and bay leaf; cover. Simmer 15 minutes to blend flavors. Remove bay leaf. Spoon onto split hamburger buns.
Note—Carry meat mixture in its kettle to reheat on grill at your eating spot. Or, if you're not taking a grill, cover kettle tightly and wrap in several thicknesses of newspaper. Food will stay hot for at least 30 minutes.

Garden Potato Salad

Mixed vegetable salad with bacon

Makes 8 servings.

6 medium-size potatoes, pared and diced
2 packages (10 ounces each) frozen lima beans
½ pound sliced bacon
1 tablespoon sugar
1½ teaspoons salt
¼ teaspoon pepper
3 tablespoons cider vinegar
3 tablespoons water
1 cup sliced radishes

1 Cook potatoes, covered, with frozen lima beans in boiling salted water in a large saucepan 10 minutes, or until both vegetables are tender; drain. Place in a large bowl.
2 Cut bacon slices crosswise into quarters. Sauté until crisp in a medium-size frying pan; remove and drain on paper toweling.
3 Pour all drippings from frying pan, then measure 3 tablespoonfuls and return to pan; stir in sugar, salt, pepper, vinegar and water; heat to boiling. Pour over vegetables; toss lightly to mix. Just before serving, arrange radish slices, overlapping, around top; mound bacon in center.
Note—To carry to your picnic, bundle cooked bacon and sliced radishes in separate plastic bags, ready to arrange atop salad just before serving.

Calico Vegetable Crunch

Makes 8 servings

2 cups thinly sliced yellow squash
2 cups thinly sliced zucchini
2 cups diced green pepper
1 pint cherry tomatoes, stemmed and halved
½ cup bottled herb-and-garlic French dressing
1 teaspoon salt

Combine vegetables in a large bowl or plastic container; drizzle with dressing and sprinkle

(continued)

If the seashore isn't near, set up this **July 4th Picnic Buffet** in your dining room

with salt. Toss lightly until vegetables are evenly coated.

Note: If your eating spot is more than 30 minutes away, place dressing in a separate container for easy carrying and toss vegetables with dressing just before serving.

Sugar-Crunch Squares

Nibble-type cake to accompany the punch

Bake at 350° for 40 minutes.
Makes one 13x9x2-inch loaf.

CAKE
3⅜ cups sifted all-purpose flour
4½ teaspoons baking powder
 1 teaspoon salt
 ¾ cup (1½ sticks) butter or margarine
1½ cups sugar
 2 eggs
1½ teaspoons vanilla
 1 cup plus 2 tablespoons milk

TOPPING
 ¾ cup sifted all-purpose flour
 ¾ cup firmly packed light brown sugar
 ½ teaspoon cinnamon
   Pinch of cloves
 ⅓ cup butter or margarine
 1 cup chopped walnuts or pecans
   10X (confectioners' powdered) sugar (decoration)

1 Make cake: Sift flour, baking powder and salt onto wax paper.
2 Cream butter or margarine with sugar until fluffy in a medium-size bowl; beat in eggs and vanilla.
3 Blend in dry ingredients, alternately with milk, just until smooth. Pour into a greased baking pan, 13x9x2.
4 Bake in a moderate oven (350°) 25 minutes; remove from oven. (Leave heat on.)
5 Make topping while cake bakes: Combine flour, sugar and spices in a small bowl; cut in butter or margarine until mixture is crumbly. Stir in nuts.
6 Sprinkle over partly baked cake; return to oven at once and bake 15 minutes longer or until golden on top and cake springs back when lightly pressed with fingertip. *(continued)*

7 Cool at least 5 minutes on wire rack. To decorate, lay 1-inch strips of wax paper or foil across top of cake, on the diagonal and about 1-inch apart. Dust 10X sugar over cake. Remove paper strips. To serve, cut in large squares.

Brown-Eyed Susans

Chocolate is the trick ingredient that makes these brown-eyed

Bake at 400° for 8 minutes.
Makes 24 large cookies.

  5 cups sifted all-purpose flour
  1 teaspoon baking powder
  ¼ teaspoon salt
1½ cups (3 sticks) butter or margarine
  2 cups granulated sugar
  3 eggs
  2 teaspoons grated lemon rind
  2 tablespoons lemon juice
  ½ cup semisweet-chocolate pieces
    Yellow decorating sugar

1 Sift flour, baking powder and salt onto wax paper.
2 Cream butter or margarine with granulated sugar until fluffy-light in a large bowl; beat in eggs, 1 at a time, until well blended; stir in lemon rind and lemon juice.
3 Stir in flour mixture, a third at a time, blending well to make a stiff dough. Chill at least an hour, or until dough is firm enough to handle. (Overnight is even better.)
4 Roll, 3 tablespoonfuls at a time, into balls between palms of hands. Place, 3 inches apart, on greased large cookie sheets. To flatten cookies and shape petals easily: Use your shortening or coffee can with plastic lid attached. Grease lid and dip in additional granulated sugar, then press balls of dough to ¼-inch thickness. Push edge of dough in slightly every 1½ inches with fingertip.
5 Press 3 semisweet-chocolate pieces in center of each round; sprinkle generously with yellow sugar.
6 Bake in hot oven (400°) 8 minutes, or until firm and lightly browned around edges. Remove from cookie sheets with a spatula; let cool completely on wire racks.
Note: Pack cookies in a sturdy box lined with crumpled wax paper or transparent wrap.

Pitcher Punch

Keep chilled for a cool thirst quencher at your picnic-buffet

Makes 8 servings, about 1 cup each.

1 can (6 ounces) frozen concentrate for Hawaiian punch, thawed
1 bottle (32 ounces) apple juice
1 cup water
  Ice cubes

Mix concentrated punch, apple juice and water in a large pitcher. Pour over ice cubes in tall glasses.
Note: Mix beverage at home and carry in a keep-cold jug. Or carry punch and apple juice in their containers, ready for mixing at your picnic spot.

MEMORABLE THANKSGIVING BUFFET

Lobster Bisque with Wheat Crackers
Roast Ribs of Beef
Holiday Roast Turkey
Scalloped Oyster Stuffing   Giblet Gravy
Golden Potato Cones   Yam Puff
Browned Onions in Squash Boats
Green Beans Parisienne
Lime Relish Baskets
Whitecap Cranberry Crown
Parker House Rolls
Dessert (of your choosing)

Lobster Bisque

Start off the meal right with this thick bisque

Makes 8 servings.

2 cans (about 6 ounces each) lobster meat
1 medium-size onion, chopped (½ cup)
¾ cup (1½ sticks) butter or margarine
¾ cup sifted all-purpose flour
2 cans (10½ ounces each) condensed chicken broth
¾ cup dry sherry
3 cups light cream or table cream
2 tablespoons tomato paste (from a 6-ounce can)
½ teaspoon salt
  Dash of pepper

1 Drain lobster; remove any bony tissue. Set aside several large pieces for garnish, then dice remainder.
2 Sauté onion in butter or margarine until soft in a large saucepan; stir in flour. Cook, stirring constantly, until bubbly.
3 Stir in chicken broth; continue cooking and stirring until mixture thickens and boils 1 minute. Stir in diced lobster and sherry; cover; simmer 20 minutes.
4 Blend in cream, tomato paste, salt and pepper; heat *slowly* just until hot. Ladle into a tureen; float saved pieces of lobster on top. Serve with wheat crackers, if you wish.

Holiday Roast Turkey

This traditional dish speaks for itself

Roast at 325° about 4 hours.

For 8 servings, plus some left for another meal, buy a turkey weighing about 12 pounds.

If you buy a regular fresh or frozen turkey, follow directions below for thawing, if needed, stuffing and roasting.
To thaw: Keep bird in its original wrapper and store in your refrigerator, allowing from 2 to 3 days. Remove giblets and neck from body or neck cavity; wash and cook for GIBLET GRAVY *(recipe follows)*. Rinse inside of turkey with cold water; drain well. Store, lightly covered, in refrigerator until ready to stuff and roast.
To stuff: Make SCALLOPED OYSTER STUFFING *(recipe follows)*, but do not put into bird until just before roasting time. Sprinkle inside of bird lightly with plain or seasoned salt, then lightly stuff neck cavity. Smooth neck skin over stuffing and skewer to back of bird. Twist wing tips until they rest flat against skewered neck skin. Next stuff body cavity. If your turkey comes "tucked," slide legs out, stuff bird lightly, then slip legs back in place. If your turkey is not a "tucked" type, lace opening together with poultry pins or skewers and string and truss legs close to body.
To roast: Brush stuffed bird all over with melted butter or margarine. (You'll need about 6 tablespoons [¾ stick].) Place, breast side up, in roasting pan—on a rack, if you wish—but do not add water or cover pan. If using a meat thermometer, stick bulb into the center of a thigh without touching bone. Roast in slow oven (325°) for time suggested on turkey wrapper, or about 4 hours for an about-12-pounder, or until thermometer registers 185°. After bird has been in the oven about 30 minutes, brush again with melted butter. During rest of roasting time, baste every half hour with buttery drippings in pan.
To test for doneness: Start testing 30 minutes before roasting time is up. Protecting your fingers with paper toweling, squeeze meaty part of thigh. It should feel soft. Now move drumstick up and down. It should twist and move easily. When turkey is done, place it on a heated platter and keep warm while making gravy. (Turkey slices more easily and neatly if allowed to stand for 15 to 20 minutes.) Garnish platter with chicory or curly endive and LIME RELISH BASKETS *(recipe follows)*. Carve bird and serve.

Scalloped Oyster Stuffing

A change from a traditional bread stuffing

Makes about 10 cups or enough to stuff a 12- pound turkey.

1 medium-size onion, diced (½ cup)
1 cup thinly sliced celery
1 cup (2 sticks) butter or margarine
2 cans (8 ounces each) oysters
1 cup light cream or table cream
¼ cup chopped parsley
½ teaspoon salt
¼ teaspoon pepper
3 packages (3½ ounces each) unsalted soda crackers, coarsely crushed

1 Sauté onion and celery in butter or margarine until soft in a small saucepan; remove from heat.
2 Drain liquid from oysters into onion mixture; stir in cream, parsley, salt and pepper.
3 Combine oysters and crackers in a large bowl; drizzle onion mixture over top; toss lightly to mix. Let stand about 5 minutes, or until liquid is absorbed. Cover and chill until ready to stuff into turkey.

Giblet Gravy

Choice gravy that helps make use of the whole bird

Makes about 4 cups.

Combine turkey giblets (except liver) and neck with 1 medium-size onion, chopped; a few celery tops; 1 teaspoon salt; 1 bay leaf; and 4 cups water in a medium-size saucepan; cover. Sim-
(continued)

Not everyone has a log cabin, but almost anyone can put together this **Memorable Thanksgiving Buffet,** that has Pilgrim overtones.

mer 1 hour and 40 minutes; add liver. Simmer 20 minutes longer, or until meat is tender. Strain broth; measure; add water, if needed, to make 4 cups. Chop giblets fine and stir into broth. Cool, then chill until ready to make gravy. After turkey has been removed from roasting pan, remove rack, if used; tip pan and let fat rise in one corner. Pour all fat into a cup, leaving juices in pan. Measure 8 tablespoons fat and return to pan; blend in ½ cup flour. Cook, stirring constantly, just until bubbly. Stir in the 4 cups broth and giblets. Continue cooking and stirring, scraping baked-on juices from bottom and sides of pan, until gravy thickens and boils 1 minute. Season to taste with salt and pepper; stir in a little bottled gravy coloring to darken, if you wish.

Golden Potato Cones

Surprise golden-fried potato cones—sure to please

Makes 8 servings.

Instant mashed potatoes
Butter or margarine
Salt
Water
2 eggs, separated
½ cup sifted all-purpose flour
1 cup sliced blanched almonds
Vegetable shortening or vegetable oil for frying

1 Prepare 4 cups instant mashed potatoes with butter or margarine, salt and water in a large saucepan, following label directions and omitting milk; beat in egg yolks. Divide into 8 even mounds; shape each into a cone.
2 Beat egg whites slightly in a pie plate; spread flour and almonds on separate pieces of wax paper.
3 Carefully roll each potato cone in flour, then in beaten egg white and almonds; stand on a plate; chill.
4 Melt enough vegetable shortening or pour vegetable oil into a large frying pan to fill two-thirds full; heat to 360°.
5 Fry potato cones, two or three at a time, turning once, 2 minutes, or until golden. Lift

(continued)

out with a slotted pancake turner; drain on paper toweling. Serve hot.
Note: Potatoes may be fried several hours ahead, if you wish. Just before serving, place on a cookie sheet. Reheat in slow oven (325°) 20 minutes.

Yam Puff

A traditional accompaniment for the traditional bird

Bake at 325° for 1 hour and 10 minutes.
Makes 8 servings.

6 large yams or sweet potatoes
4 eggs, separated
4 tablespoons (½ stick) butter or margarine
1 cup light cream or table cream
3 tablespoons sugar
1 tablespoon grated orange peel
½ teaspoon ground cinnamon
¼ teaspoon ground nutmeg

1 Cook yams or sweet potatoes in boiling salted water in a large saucepan 30 minutes, or until tender; drain. Cool until easy to handle, then peel; place in a large bowl.
2 While potatoes cool, beat egg whites until they stand in firm peaks in a medium-size bowl.
3 Break up potatoes with a fork, then beat in egg yolks, butter or margarine, cream, sugar, orange peel, cinnamon and nutmeg; continue beating until fluffy-light. Fold in beaten egg whites. Spoon into a greased 8-cup baking dish.
4 Bake in slow oven (325°) 1 hour and 10 minutes, or until slightly puffed and firm. Garnish with orange slices, if you wish.

Browned Onions in Squash Boats

Nearly every dish is sculptured in this creative menu—including these squash boats

Makes 8 servings.

4 tablespoons (½ stick) butter or margarine
2 tablespoons vegetable oil
40 small white onions (about 2 pounds), peeled
2 envelopes instant beef broth
   OR: 2 beef-flavor bouillon cubes
1 teaspoon dried parsley flakes
¼ teaspoon garlic powder
¼ teaspoon leaf thyme, crumbled

1 cup water
   STEAMED SQUASH (recipe follows)

1 Melt butter or margarine with vegetable oil in a large frying pan; stir in onions. Sauté, turning often, 10 minutes, or until golden.
2 Stir in beef broth, parsley, garlic powder, thyme and water; heat to boiling; cover. Simmer 30 minutes, or until tender.
3 Spoon onions and sauce into STEAMED QUASH. Sprinkle onions with paprika, if desired.

STEAMED SQUASH

Trim 4 small acorn squashes; halve each lengthwise; scoop out seeds. Place halves, cut sides down, in two large frying pans; pour boiling water into each pan to a depth of ½ inch; cover. Steam 30 minutes, or until squashes are tender; drain. Brush hollows with melted butter or margarine.

Lime Relish Baskets

The lime basket is filled with a delightful vegetable combination

Makes 8 servings.

8 large limes
1 jar (6 ounces) marinated artichoke hearts
1 can (12 or 16 ounces) whole-kernel corn, drained
1 can or jar (4 ounces) pimientos, drained and diced
1 tablespoon grated onion
2 tablespoons sugar
¼ teaspoon salt

1 Make lime baskets this way: Mark a guideline lengthwise around center of lime with the tip of a knife, then mark off a ¼-inch-wide strip across the top for handle. Cut out sections between marks and remove remaining lime pulp from bottom. Wrap baskets in foil or transparent wrap and chill.
2 Dice enough of the lime pulp to measure ¼ cup; place in a medium-size bowl. (Use remainder for punch or for flavoring fruit cup.) Drain liquid from artichoke hearts into bowl with lime; chop artichokes and add with corn, pimientos, onion, sugar and salt; toss lightly to mix. Chill at least 6 hours to season.

3 When ready to serve, trim a thin slice from bottom of each lime basket, if needed, to make basket stand flat; spoon corn mixture into baskets.

Green Beans Parisienne

There's plenty of color in this menu—including these sprightly green beans

Makes 8 servings.

*3 packages (9 ounces each) frozen cut green
  beans
1 cup thinly sliced celery
4 tablespoons (½ stick) butter or margarine
¼ cup water
1 teaspoon salt
4 medium-size mushrooms, trimmed and
  sliced*

1 Combine green beans, celery, butter or margarine, water and salt in a medium-size frying pan. Heat to boiling; cover.
2 Cook 8 minutes; add mushrooms. Cook 2 minutes longer, or just until beans are tender.
3 Spoon into a heated serving bowl; drizzle buttery sauce from pan over top.

Whitecap Cranberry Crown

A molded dessert with a delicious pear surprise

Makes 8 servings.

*4 envelopes unflavored gelatin
1 bottle (48 ounces) cranberry-apple drink
¼ cup mayonnaise or salad dressing
¼ cup dairy sour cream
3 ripe pears, pared, quartered, cored, and
  diced
  Watercress*

1 Soften gelatin in 2 cups of the cranberry-apple drink in a medium-size saucepan. Heat slowly, stirring constantly, until gelatin dissolves; remove from heat. Stir in remaining 4 cups cranberry-apple drink.
2 Measure ½ cup of the gelatin mixture into a small bowl; set aside. Chill remaining gelatin mixture 50 minutes, or until as thick as unbeaten egg white.
3 Beat mayonnaise or salad dressing and sour cream into the ½-cup gelatin mixture; pour into an 8-cup tube mold.

4 Place mold in a pan of ice and water to speed setting; chill just until sticky firm.
5 Fold pears into thickened gelatin mixture in saucepan; carefully spoon over dressing layer in mold. Remove from ice and water. Chill in refrigerator at least 6 hours, or overnight.
6 When ready to unmold, run a sharp-tip, thin-blade knife around top of salad, then dip mold *very quickly* in and out of hot water. Cover mold with a large serving plate; turn upside down, then gently lift off mold. Garnish center of salad and plate with watercress.

DOWN HOME CHRISTMAS BUFFET

King's Soup*
Soda Crackers
Christmas Goose with Orange Sauce*
Whipped Potatoes
Whole Cauliflower and Green Beans
Platter*
Supreme Sauce*
Colonial Turnip Bowl*
Spicy Cranberry Mold*
Turnip - Carrot - Celery Sticks
Yuletide Saffron Crown*
Rum Pumpkin Pie*
Old-Fashioned Mince Pie*
Sweet Cider   Madeira   Claret
Festive Holiday Punch*
Baker Family Christmas Cookies*
Lillyan Green's Chocolate Cookies*

King's Soup

A recipe for this creamy version of onion soup was published in "The Lady's Companion" in 1753 in the Virginia Colony

Makes 8 servings.

*2 large Bermuda onions, thinly sliced
½ cup (1 stick) butter or margarine
2 teaspoons salt
¼ teaspoon ground mace
¼ teaspoon white pepper
4 cups milk
2 cups light cream
2 egg yolks
  Chopped parsley*

1 Sauté onion slices in butter or margarine until very soft, *but not brown,* in a soup kettle; stir in salt, mace and white pepper; cook 1 minute.
(continued)

2 Add milk and cream and simmer 30 minutes. Beat egg yolks in a small bowl; blend in 1 cup hot soup; stir into kettle; cook, stirring constantly, 5 minutes. Ladle into heated soup tureen and garnish with chopped parsley.

Hostess Tip: This soup is even more flavorful if made the day before and chilled until 30 minutes before serving time. Heat slowly, but do not allow to boil, or soup will curdle.

Christmas Goose with Orange Sauce

Geese were one of the domesticated birds brought from England to Long Island in the 1700's

Roast at 400° for 1 hour,
then at 325° for 1½ hours.
Makes 8 servings plus leftovers.

1 frozen goose (8 to 10 pounds) thawed
  Salt and pepper
1 small onion, chopped (¼ cup)
¼ cup chopped carrot
¼ cup chopped celery
½ cup sugar
3 tablespoons cider vinegar
1 tablespoon grated orange rind
2 cups orange juice
3 tablespoons cornstarch
⅓ cup cold water
¼ cup orange liqueur
2 California oranges, sectioned

1 Remove neck and giblets from goose and cook immediately for goose broth. Remove excess fat from body cavity and neck skin. Season cavity with salt and pepper; truss goose.
2 Place goose, breast-side up, on a rack in a large roasting pan. Insert a meat thermometer into the inside thigh muscle, if you wish.
3 Roast in hot oven (400°) 1 hour, removing accumulated fat from roasting pan with a bulb baster every 30 minutes; reduce oven temperature to slow (325°); roast 1 hour longer; add onion, carrot and celery; roast ½ hour longer, or until temperature on the meat thermometer reaches 108° and drumstick moves easily.
4 Remove goose from roasting pan to heated platter and keep warm; pour off fat from roasting pan.
5 Sprinkle sugar over bottom of a small heavy saucepan; shake over medium heat until sugar melts and turns a light brown; stir in vinegar carefully, as it will sizzle when mixed with the hot sugar.

6 Stir sugar mixture into roasting pan with orange rind and juice. Cook, stirring up all the baked-on pan juices, until mixture bubbles. Stir in a mixture of cornstarch and cold water; cook, stirring constantly, 1 minute. Strain into a medium-size saucepan. Add orange liqueur and orange sections; simmer 5 minutes. Serve in heated gravy boat with sliced goose.

Cook's Tip: Don't waste the goose fat, but keep to use in making leftover goose dishes or for a flavorful cooking fat. Melt down solid pieces of goose fat and add to the fat accumulated during roasting; strain through cheesecloth into a glass jar with a screw top; refrigerate and use within 1 month.

Whole Cauliflower and Green Bean Platter

Cauliflower is served with a wreath of green beans and a crown of Supreme Sauce

Makes 8 servings.

1 large cauliflower, trimmed
2 tablespoons lemon juice
1 pound green beans, tipped
1 teaspoon leaf basil, crumbled
1 teaspoon sugar
1 teaspoon salt
  SUPREME SAUCE (recipe follows)

1 Cook cauliflower with lemon juice in salted boiling water in a large skillet 30 minutes, or until crisply tender when pierced with the tip of a paring knife; remove with pancake turner to heated serving platter and keep warm.
2 Cook green beans with basil, sugar and salt in boiling water in a large saucepan 15 minutes, or until crisply tender. Remove with slotted spoon and arrange around cauliflower. Serve SUPREME SAUCE in heated sauce dish.

Supreme Sauce

Makes about 2½ cups.

1 tablespoon finely chopped onion
⅓ cup butter or margarine
⅓ cup all-purpose flour
½ teaspoon salt
⅛ teaspoon pepper
1 envelope or teaspoon instant chicken broth
2 cups milk

This year save mother the extra effort of setting out a table by creating an informal **Down Home Christmas Buffet.**

4 tablespoons grated Parmesan cheese
2 tablespoons heavy cream

1 Sauté onions in butter or margarine just until soft in a small heavy saucepan; stir in flour, salt and pepper; cook, stirring constantly over low heat, just until mixture bubbles; add instant chicken broth.
2 Stir in milk slowly; continue cooking and stirring until sauce thickens and bubbles 3 minutes. Stir in cheese and cream. Keep warm over low heat.

Colonial Turnip Bowl

Maple syrup adds an authentic touch to this recipe that lifts everyday turnip into festive fare

Makes 8 servings.

1 large yellow turnip
2 teaspoons sugar
¼ cup (½ stick) butter or margarine
¼ cup maple syrup or maple-flavored pancake syrup
1 teaspoon salt
¼ teaspoon white pepper

1 Cut turnip in half with a sharp heavy knife; cut into ¾-inch slices; pare skin from slices; cube slices.
2 Cover turnip cubes with water in a large saucepan; sprinkle with sugar; bring to boiling; lower heat; simmer 45 minutes, or until turnip is tender; drain in colander.
3 Melt butter or margarine in same saucepan; stir in syrup, salt and pepper and heat until bubbling; return turnip to saucepan and toss to coat well with maple syrup mixture.
Cook's Tip: Turnips can be spooned into vegetable dish and kept in warm oven until serving time.

Spicy Cranberry Mold

It's perfect with poultry and game

Makes one 6-cup mold.

4 cups (1 pound) fresh cranberries
1 cup seedless raisins
1⅔ cups sugar
1 tablespoon ground cinnamon
1½ teaspoons ground ginger

(continued)

¼ *teaspoon ground cloves*
1 *cup water*
1 *medium-size onion, chopped (½ cup)*
1 *medium-size apple, pared, quartered, cored and chopped*
½ *cup thinly sliced celery*
1 *package (6 ounces) cherry-flavored gelatin*

1 Combine cranberries, raisins, sugar, cinnamon, ginger, cloves and water in a large saucepan. Simmer 15 minutes, or until cranberries pop.
2 Stir in onion, apple and celery; simmer 15 minutes, or until thick. Stir in cherry gelatin until gelatin dissolves. Pour into a 6-cup mold. Chill until firm.
3 To serve: Unmold gelatin by running a sharp-tipped, thin-bladed knife around edge of bowl; then dip mold *quickly* in and out of a pan of hot water; invert onto serving plate and return to refrigerator until serving time.

Yuletide Saffron Crown

Saffron is a spice that gives a golden color as well as flavor to breads

Bake at 400° for 30 to 40 minutes.
Makes one 10-inch tube.

1 *envelope active dry yeast*
¼ *cup very warm water*
⅓ *cup sugar*
⅓ *cup milk, heated and cooled*
3 *cups all-purpose flour*
6 *eggs, slightly beaten*
  Few strands saffron, crushed
½ *cup (1 stick) butter or margarine, melted*
1 *teaspoon salt*

1 Sprinkle yeast into very warm water in a large bowl. ("Very warm" water should feel comfortably warm when dropped on wrist.) Stir until yeast dissolves, then stir in 1 tablespoon of the sugar; allow to stand until mixture bubbles, about 10 minutes.
2 Stir in milk, flour, eggs and saffron. Beat 5 minutes with electric mixer on medium speed, or until dough is smooth and elastic; stir in melted butter or margarine.
3 Cover with clean towel; let rise in warm place, away from draft, 1 hour, or until double in bulk.
4 Stir dough down; beat in remaining sugar and salt. (Dough will be spongy-soft.) Spoon into greased fancy 12-cup tube mold.
5 Cover; let rise in warm place, away from draft, 30 minutes, or until double in bulk.

6 Bake in hot oven (400°) 30 to 40 minutes, or until richly golden. Cool in mold 5 minutes; turn out onto wire rack; cool completely. Sprinkle with 10X sugar, just before serving and garnish with a ring of sliced almonds, if you wish.

Rum Pumpkin Pie

Mrs. Elizabeth Steidel of Long Island has found a way to blend two favorites from Colonial Days into one delicious pie

Bake at 425° for 45 minutes.
Makes one 9-inch pie.

½ *package pie crust mix*
1 *can (1 pound) pumpkin*
1 *cup firmly packed dark brown sugar*
3 *eggs, slightly beaten*
1½ *cups milk, scalded*
¼ *cup rum*
1 *tablespoon molasses*
½ *teaspoon ground cinnamon*
¼ *teaspoon ground cloves*
¼ *teaspoon ground ginger*
¼ *teaspoon salt*

1 Prepare pie crust, following label directions, or make pastry from your favorite single-crust recipe. Roll out on a lightly-floured pastry cloth or board to a 12-inch round; fit into a 9-inch pie plate. Trim overhang to ½ inch; turn under; flute to make a stand-up edge.
2 Combine pumpkin, sugar, eggs, milk, rum, molasses, cinnamon, cloves, ginger and salt in a large bowl. Mix with a wire whip until well blended.
3 Place prepared pie shell on rack in oven; pour filling into pie up to pastry rim. (Note: If you are using a frozen 9-inch pie shell, you will have too much filling for shell. Simply pour remaining pumpkin mixture into custard cups and place in a pan; pour in hot water to a depth of 1-inch. Bake along with pie.)
4 Bake in hot oven (425°) 45 minutes, or until pie is set around edge, but still soft near center. (Note: Should pastry begin to get too brown during baking, lower heat to moderate oven (350°) for remaining cooking time).

Old-Fashioned Mince Pie

Rich, savory mincemeat has made this dessert a favorite holiday tradition

Bake at 400° for 30 minutes.
Makes one 9-inch pie.

1 package pie crust mix
4 cups OLD-FASHIONED MINCEMEAT (recipe follows)
1 medium-size apple, chopped (1 cup)
SOFT CHEDDAR SPREAD (recipe follows)

1 Prepare pie crust mix, following label directions, or make pastry from your own favorite two-crust recipe. Roll out half to a 12-inch round on lightly-floured pastry cloth or board; fit into a 9-inch pie plate.
2 Combine OLD-FASHIONED MINCEMEAT and apple in medium-size bowl; pour into prepared shell.
3 Roll out remaining pastry to a rectangle about 12x8; cut into 10 long strips, each about ¾-inch wide, with pastry wheel or knife. Weave strips over filling to make a crisscross top; trim ends and bottom overhang to ½ inch; turn up over edge; flute.
4 Bake in hot oven (400°) 30 minutes, or until juices bubble up and crust is golden. Serve warm with SOFT CHEDDAR SPREAD.
Cook's Tip: To make this pie the speedy new-fashioned way, substitute 1 jar (about 1 pound, 13 ounces) ready-to-use mincemeat or 1 package (9 ounces) condensed mincemeat, reconstituted following label directions. Then add chopped apple, the same as in homemade mincemeat.

SOFT CHEDDAR SPREAD
Grate ½ pound sharp Cheddar cheese (2 cups) into medium-size bowl. Add 1 package (8 ounces) cream cheese, softened, and a dash of cayenne pepper; beat until fluffy-light. Spoon into serving bowl; chill. (This spread keeps well, but should be served at room temperature for best flavor.) Makes about 2 cups.

Old-Fashioned Mincemeat

A rich, spice-laden filling for our traditional Christmas pie

Makes 8 cups.

1 pound boneless lean beef chuck, finely diced

2½ cups water
4 medium-size apples, (4 cups) chopped
1 package (15 ounces) seedless raisins
1 package (11 ounces) dried currants
1 jar (4 ounces) candied citron
1¾ cups firmly packed brown sugar
½ cup light molasses
½ cup (1 stick) butter or margarine
1 teaspoon grated lemon rind
2 tablespoons lemon juice
2 teaspoons salt
2 teaspoons ground cinnamon
1 teaspoon ground mace
½ teaspoon ground cloves
1½ cups sweet cider
½ cup rum or dry sherry

1 Simmer beef in water 30 minutes in a large kettle. Stir in apples, raisins, currants, citron, brown sugar, molasses, butter or margarine, lemon rind and juice, salt, cinnamon, mace, cloves, cider, rum or sherry. Simmer, stirring often, 1 hour, or until slightly thickened.
2 Ladle into 2 one-quart jars or a large glass or pottery bowl; cool; cover tightly. Store in refrigerator for at least 1 month to ripen and mellow flavor. Mincemeat will keep up to 6 months.

Festive Holiday Punch

A cheery bowl of punch was often awaiting holiday guests at Christmas-time in many eighteenth-century inns

Makes 16 punch-cup servings.

4 sugar cubes
2 large lemons
¼ teaspoon ground ginger
1 can (46 ounces) fruit juicy-red Hawaiian punch, chilled
1½ cups apple juice, chilled
1½ cups light rum
Ice block or ice cubes
Lemon slices

1 Rub sugar cubes over lemons to release oil from lemon skin; place sugar cubes in punch bowl. Squeeze enough juice from lemons to make ¼ cup; pour over sugar cubes, stir to dissolve sugar. Stir in ginger.
2 Add punch, apple juice and rum; mix well. Add ice block or ice cubes, and garnish with lemon slices, if you wish.
Hostess Tip: To make a punch bowl ice mold,
(continued)

choose a metal bowl smaller than punch bowl and about 4-cups in volume. Fill with water and freeze at least overnight. Run bowl under hot water to loosen ice block and slip into punch bowl.

Baker Family Christmas Cookies

This French family heirloom recipe is shared by Mrs. John (Mimi) Ashton in "Cooking—North Fork Style"

Bake at 375° for 10 minutes.
Makes 3 dozen.

3 egg yolks
1 cup sugar
1 cup (2 sticks) butter or margarine, softened
3½ cups all-purpose flour
½ teaspoon baking powder
½ teaspoon baking soda
½ teaspoon salt
1 container (8 ounces) dairy sour cream
Anise seeds (optional)
1 can (about 1 pound) creamy white frosting
Bottled food coloring
Assorted decorating frostings (in 4½-ounce tubes)

1 Beat egg yolks at high speed of electric mixer in a large bowl until thick; gradually beat in sugar and butter or margarine until creamy-smooth.
2 Sift in flour, baking powder, baking soda and salt alternately with sour cream; stir to make a stiff dough.
3 Roll out onto lightly-floured pastry cloth or board sprinkled with anise seeds, if desired, to a ¼-inch thickness. Cut out with your favorite 3- to 4-inch cookie cutters, or use your own patterns. Place on ungreased cookie sheets.
4 Bake in moderate oven (375°) 10 minutes, or until golden. Remove from cookie sheets to wire racks to cool completely. Spread with frosting, tinted various colors with food coloring; make outlines using various decorating tips.

Lillyan Green's Chocolate Cookies

This extra-crisp rich chocolate wafer has been a specialty of Lillyan Green every Christmas for years

Bake at 350° for 7 minutes.
Makes 4 dozen.

½ cup (1 stick) butter or margarine
1 cup sugar

1 egg
1 square unsweetened chocolate, melted
1 cup all-purpose flour
½ teaspoon vanilla

1 Cream butter or margarine and sugar together until light and fluffy in a large bowl with electric mixer at high speed.
2 Beat in egg and chocolate until well blended; stir in flour and vanilla to make a soft dough. Shape dough into a 2½-inch wide roll on sheet of wax paper; wrap in wax paper. Freeze overnight, or until ready to bake.
3 Cut frozen dough into ¼-inch thick slices with a very sharp knife and arrange on ungreased cookie sheets.
4 Bake in moderate oven (350°) 7 minutes, or until cookies are firm. Transfer to wire racks with pancake turner to cool. Store in a metal tin with a tight-fitting lid.

CONTINENTAL CHRISTMAS BUFFET

Festive Pâté en Croûte
Celery Hearts   Olives
Herbed Beef Roast
Crown Roast of Pork
Vegetable Bouquet Platter
Swiss Scalloped Potatoes
Cucumber-Lime Cream Mold
Hot Croissants   Butter Balls
Christmas Green Mint Pie
Old English Trifle
Fruits in Snow
Cream Mints   Salted Nuts
Coffee

Festive Pâté en Croûte

A gourmet treat for this special occasion

Bake at 325° for 1½ hours,
then at 425° for 45 minutes.
Makes 8 to 12 servings.

½ pound sliced bacon
1 pound chicken livers
¼ cup sifted all-purpose flour
2 teaspoons salt
½ teaspoon pepper
1 teaspoon leaf thyme, crumbled
4 tablespoons light cream or table cream
3 tablespoons Cognac

Scrooge would have had a change of heart had he seen this elegant Christmas buffet: **Crown Roast of Pork, Swiss Scalloped Potatoes, Cucumber-Lime Cream Mold, Hot Croissants, Christmas Green Mint Pie,** and **Old English Trifle.**

1½ pounds ground veal
1 pound ground pork
2 eggs
PÂTÉ PASTRY (recipe follows)

1 Line the bottom and sides of an 8¼-inch pâte mold or a 9x5x3-inch loaf pan with bacon slices.
2 Place half of the chicken livers in an electric blender container. Whirl until smooth, about 1 minute. Add remaining chicken livers and whirl again until smooth.

3 Add flour, salt, pepper, thyme, cream and Cognac to chicken livers and blend until smooth. (If you don't have a blender, put chicken livers through a food grinder, using the fine blade, then stir in other ingredients in a medium-size bowl.)
4 Mix ground veal and pork together until smooth in a large bowl. Beat eggs in a small bowl, reserving 2 tablespoons for Step 10. Beat remaining beaten egg and the liver mixture into

(continued)

ground meats to make a very smooth mixture. Pour all but 1 cup of meat mixture into prepared mold. Chill remaining cup of mixture for Step 8. Top meat mixture in mold with remaining bacon strips. Place mold in a shallow baking pan.

5 Bake in slow oven (325°) 1½ hours; remove from oven. Cool in mold on a wire rack, placing a heavy dish over pâté to weigh it down. When cool, remove weight, then slip pins off sides of mold; remove mold from pâté. For loaf pan, turn pâté out of pan; remove all bacon strips. (Pâté mixture may be prepared to this step, then refrigerated, one or two days ahead.)

6 Wash, dry and grease the sides of mold; slip pins into place and place mold on a shallow baking pan. (Or line a 9x5x3-inch loaf pan with foil, leaving a 1-inch overhang on all sides; grease foil.)

7 Roll out ⅔ of PÂTÉ PASTRY to a 18x 14-inch oval on a lightly floured pastry cloth or board. Fold pastry in half and fit into bottom and up sides of pâté mold. (Or roll out pastry to a 16x12-rectangle for loaf pan.)

8 Fit baked pâté into pastry-lined mold, loosening pins on sides of mold for ease of fitting; tighten pins into place. Spread cooked pâté with reserved meat mixture.

9 Roll out remaining PÂTÉ PASTRY to an 11x7-inch oval. Using pâté mold base as a guide, cut a top crust; make slits in center of crust; place on top of pâté. (Or roll out pastry to 10x6-inch rectangle for loaf pan.)

10 Beat reserved 2 tablespoons egg with 2 tablespoons of water in a cup. Brush pastry with egg wash.

11 Trim pastry overhang to ½ inch; turn edge up, flush with rim; press into top crust. Make pastry decorations with trims, using tiny hors d'oeuvres cutters; brush with egg wash.

12 Bake in hot oven (425°) 30 minutes. Remove from oven and remove pâté-mold sides. Brush top and sides of pastry with egg wash; cover top crust with aluminum foil. (Or lift pâté out of loaf pan, using overhanging foil as lifters, then remove foil.)

13 Bake in hot oven (425°) 15 minutes longer, or until pastry is golden. Serve warm or cold.

Pâté Pastry

Makes crust and trims for 1 pâté

3½ cups sifted all-purpose flour
1 teaspoon salt
1 cup (2 sticks) butter or margarine
2 eggs, beaten
3 tablespoons ice water

1 Sift flour and salt into a large bowl. Cut in butter or margarine until crumbly with a pastry blender.

2 Make a well in center of mixture and add beaten eggs and water. Stir with a fork to make a stiff pastry.

3 Turn out onto a lightly floured pastry cloth or board and knead 10 times. Wrap in foil or plastic wrap and chill at least 2 hours.

Herbed Beef Roast

So rich and flavorful, you'll want to serve leftovers during the festive season

Roast at 325° for 3 hours.
Makes 8 servings.

1 rolled boned rib roast of beef, weighing about 8 pounds
½ cup unsifted all-purpose flour
4 tablespoons leaf rosemary, crumbled
2 tablespoons dry mustard
2 tablespoons seasoned salt
2 teaspoons seasoned pepper

1 Preheat oven to slow (325°).

2 Wipe roast with wet paper toweling, leaving surface very moist.

3 Combine flour, rosemary, mustard, seasoned salt and seasoned pepper in a small bowl. Sprinkle evenly over moist surface of meat, patting on firmly with palms of hands.

4 Place roast, fat side up, on rack in shallow roasting pan; do not add water or cover pan. Insert meat thermometer into roast so the bulb end reaches the center of the meat and does not rest in fat.

5 Roast 3 hours, or until thermometer registers 140°—rare; or 160°—medium.

6 Remove meat from oven; place on a heated serving platter. Cover loosely with foil; let stand 20 minutes in a warm place. (This makes roast easier to slice.) Turn roast meat side up. Carve across the grain, cutting strings as you carve.

Crown Roast of Pork

Start with a large crown pork roast and build an eye-catching buffet around it

Roast at 325° for 3 hours.
Makes 8 servings.

1 sixteen- to eighteen-chop crown pork roast
1 large onion, chopped (1 cup)
1 cup chopped celery
6 tablespoons (¾ stick) butter or margarine
1 can (6 ounces) frozen orange juice concentrate, thawed
4 cups cubed white bread (8 slices)
1 teaspoon salt
¼ teaspoon fennel seed, crushed
⅛ teaspoon pepper
1 pound cranberries, washed and stemmed
½ cup honey
    Preserved kumquats
    Watercress
    CRANBERRY ORANGE CUPS (recipe follows)

1 Preheat oven to slow (325°).
2 Place roast, rib ends up, on a piece of foil in a shallow roasting pan. Wrap ends of bones with foil. Insert meat thermometer into roast so bulb end reaches the center of one chop without touching bone.
3 Roast 2 hours, or until thermometer registers 160°.
4 While roast cooks, sauté onions and celery in butter or margarine until soft in a medium-size skillet. Stir in ¼ cup of the orange juice concentrate; heat mixture to boiling; pour over bread cubes in a medium-size bowl. Add salt, fennel and pepper; toss lightly until evenly moist. Stir in 1 cup of the cranberries.
5 Spoon stuffing lightly into hollow center of roast, mounding slightly. Continue roasting pork for another 30 minutes.
6 Blend remaining orange juice with honey in a small saucepan; heat to boiling; reduce heat; simmer 2 minutes. Brush outside of roast with part of the orange mixture. Continue roasting, brushing several times with remaining orange mixture, 30 minutes, or until thermometer registers 170° and pork is tender and richly glazed.
7 Lift roast onto a heated large serving platter; remove foil. Garnish rib ends with kumquats. Frame roast with watercress and CRANBERRY ORANGE CUPS.
8 Carve between ribs into servings.

CRANBERRY ORANGE CUPS

Cut 4 small seedless oranges in half. With a small sharp knife, scallop the cut edge, then scoop out centers to make a cup. Chop centers. Heat 1½ cups sugar and 1½ cups water to boiling in a medium-size saucepan. Add chopped orange and remaining 3 cups cranberries. Cook, following label directions; cool; fill orange cups. Serve any remaining cranberry sauce separately.

Vegetable Bouquet Platter

Frozen foods let you serve vegetables out of season

Makes 8 servings.

1 large head cauliflower (about 3 pounds)
2 packages (about 9 ounces each) frozen cut green beans
2 cans (14 ounces each) small whole carrots
⅓ cup butter or margarine
2 tablespoons finely chopped parsley
1 tablespoon lemon juice
    Dash of salt

1 Trim outer green leaves from cauliflower, but leave head whole. Cook, covered, in boiling salted water in a large saucepan 30 minutes, until crisply tender.
2 While cauliflower cooks, heat carrots with their juice until bubbly in a medium-size saucepan. Cook green beans in a medium-size saucepan, following label directions.
3 Lift cauliflower from saucepan with a two-tined fork; place in center of a large heated serving platter. Drain carrots and green beans. With a slotted spoon, arrange around cauliflower.
4 Melt butter or margarine in a small saucepan; add parsley, lemon juice and salt. Pour over vegetables.

Swiss Scalloped Potatoes

The potatoes combine with Swiss cheese for this special dish

Bake at 325° for 1 hour and 45 minutes.
Makes 8 servings.

3 pounds of potatoes, pared and thinly sliced (8 cups)

(continued)

1 medium onion, grated
½ pound Swiss cheese, grated
3 eggs
2¼ cups milk
2 teaspoons salt
¼ teaspoon pepper
½ teaspoon paprika

1 Heat 3 quarts of water to boiling in a kettle; add potatoes. Cook, uncovered, 5 minutes; drain.
2 Place alternating layers of potatoes, onion and cheese in a buttered 12-cup shallow baking dish.
3 Combine eggs, milk, salt and pepper in a small bowl; beat well. Pour over potatoes. Sprinkle top with paprika. Cover baking dish with foil.
4 Bake in slow oven (325°) for 45 minutes. Remove foil; continue baking 1 hour longer, or until golden-brown.

Cucumber-Lime Cream Mold

A molded side dish you prepare ahead of time

Makes 8 servings.

3 packages (3 ounces each) lime-flavored gelatin
1½ teaspoons salt
2⅔ cups boiling water
2 tablespoons cider vinegar
3 cups dairy sour cream (1½ pints)
2 medium-size cucumbers, pared and finely chopped (2 cups)
⅔ cup chopped green onion

1 Dissolve gelatin and salt in boiling water in a large bowl. Stir in vinegar. Chill until as thick as unbeaten egg white.
2 Beat in sour cream; fold in cucumbers and onion. Pour into an 8-cup mold. Chill about 4 hours, or until firm.
3 Just before serving, loosen salad around edge with a knife; dip mold very quickly in and out of hot water. Wipe water off mold. Shake mold gently to loosen. Cover with a serving plate; turn upside down; gently lift off mold. Garnish with tiny lettuce leaves, cherry tomatoes and cucumber slices, if you wish.

Christmas Green Mint Pie

Green crème de menthe and food coloring provide the color accent

Bake at 325° for 10 minutes,
then at 450° for 4 minutes.
Makes 8 servings.

1 package (5 ounces) shortbread cookies, crushed (about 1⅓ cups)
½ cup finely chopped pecans
⅓ cup firmly packed light brown sugar
6 tablespoons (¾ stick) butter or margarine, melted
½ cup water
10 tablespoons granulated sugar
2 tablespoons green crème de menthe
1 quart vanilla ice cream, softened
½ cup cream for whipping
Few drops green food coloring
3 egg whites
⅛ teaspoon cream of tartar

1 Blend shortbread crumbs, pecans, brown sugar and butter or margarine in a medium-size bowl. Press mixture firmly over bottom and side of a 9-inch pie plate.

2 Bake in slow oven (325°) 10 minutes, or until set. Cool completely on a wire rack.

3 Combine water with 4 tablespoons of the sugar in a small saucepan; cover. Bring to boiling; uncover; continue boiling, without stirring, 7 minutes. Remove from heat; cool slightly; stir in crème de menthe; cool completely.

4 Spread half the ice cream in an even layer in cooled pie shell; cover; freeze until firm.

5 Combine cream with food coloring in a small bowl; beat until stiff Fold in 2 tablespoons of the cooled creme de menthe syrup into the cream. Spread evenly over firm ice cream in pie shell. Freeze until firm. Top with remaining ice cream. Freeze until firm. Pie may be wrapped in foil or plastic wrap, and kept frozen for a week before the buffet.

6 Beat egg whites with cream of tartar until foamy-white and double in volume in a medium-size bowl. Beat in the remaining 6 tablespoons sugar, 1 tablespoon at a time, until meringue stands in firm peaks. Pile meringue onto filling, sealing firmly to crust edge and swirling into peaks. Freeze overnight.

7 Just before serving, brown meringue until lightly golden in very hot oven (450°) for 4 minutes. Drizzle with remaining crème de menthe syrup; serve at once.

Old English Trifle

Traditionally, the British hid a penny in the trifle—for luck

Makes 8 servings.

  6 egg yolks
½ cup sugar
2¼ cups milk
  2 cups cream for whipping
¼ cup cream sherry
  2 baker's jelly rolls (about 11 ounces each)
    Red candied pineapple or red candied cherries
    Angelica or citron

1 Beat yolks slightly with sugar in the top of a double boiler. Stir in milk and 1 cup of the cream.
2 Cook, stirring constantly, over simmering water, 25 minutes, or until mixture is thickened and coats a spoon.
3 Strain custard into a medium-size bowl; cool slightly; stir in sherry.
4 Cut each jelly roll into 6 slices and line a pretty crystal serving bowl. Pour warm custard carefully over slices; cover bowl with foil or transparent wrap. Chill thoroughly, 3 hours or more.
5 To serve: Beat remaining 1 cup cream until stiff in a small bowl. Decorate top of trifle with poufs of cream. Garnish with slivers of candied pineapple or cherries and angelica or citron.

Fruits in Snow

This is an edible centerpiece.

  9 apples, various varieties and sizes
  5 pears, various varieties and sizes
  3 oranges
  2 large bunches purple grapes
  2 large bunches green grapes
  2 lemons
  2 limes
    Strawberries
    Kumquats
  2 egg whites, lightly beaten
  4 cups VANILLA SUGAR (recipe follows)
    Lemon leaves

1 Wash and dry fruits on paper toweling. Brush each piece of fruit with egg white, then sprinkle generously with VANILLA SUGAR. Allow to dry on cookie sheets. (You can place the grapes on cookie sheets, brush with egg white, and sprinkle with sugar.)
2 When ready to assemble, choose a three-tiered stand. Arrange bunches of grapes over edge of stand and place a large piece of fruit over grapes to keep them in place.
Arrange alternating colors and shapes of large fruit on stand to make a pretty composition. Place groups of strawberries and kumquats in spots for color accents. Garnish with lemon leaves.

VANILLA SUGAR
Scrape the seeds from a 4-inch length of vanilla bean. (You will find vanilla beans in a jar in the spice section of the supermarket.) Stir into 4 cups granulated sugar in a jar. Place the pod in the jar, too; cover, and let stand about a week to develop the full flavor.

Buffets For A Crowd

If your party list grows and grows—don't despair. You can easily invite more than 20 people—and for a wedding buffet, up to 100—if you plan properly. And you can do this, if you use one of the many multi-people buffets in these pages.

OUTDOOR BUFFET FOR 16

Dip-and-Chip Tray
Meat Ball Outriggers/Honolulu Heroes
Chicken Steamers
Mauna Loa Cream Tower
Hilo Fruits/Islands Sundae Sauce
Kona Cream
Fruit Punch/Brownie Rounds

Meat Ball Outriggers

Hollow loaves of bread, then heap with saucy ground-beef balls. Be sure to set out knives and forks for everyone

Makes 16 servings

4 loaves Italian bread
3 pounds ground beef
2 eggs, slightly beaten
2 tablespoons instant minced onion
3 teaspoons salt
1 teaspoon paprika
½ cup milk
2 tablespoons vegetable oil
2 tablespoons all-purpose flour
1 bottle (12 ounces) chili sauce
1 cup water
1 tablespoon light brown sugar
1 teaspoon dry mustard
Butter or margarine

1 Cut a ½-inch-thick slice from top of each loaf of bread; cut out inside to leave a ½-inch-thick boat-shape shell. Crumble enough of the insides to measure 2½ cups; save remaining with top slices to turn into croutons for another day. Cover loaves to keep them from drying out.

There's a look of the Pacific about this buffet for 16, with **Meat Ball Outriggers, Honolulu Heroes,** and **Mauna Loa Cream Tower.**

2 Combine ground beef, the 2½ cups bread crumbs, eggs, onion, salt, paprika, and milk in a large bowl; mix lightly until well-blended. Shape into tiny balls, using 1 tablespoon for each. (There should be about 110 meat balls.)
3 Brown, part at a time, in vegetable oil in a large frying pan; remove with a slotted spoon to a large bowl.
4 Stir flour into drippings in frying pan; cook, stirring constantly, just until bubbly. Stir in chili sauce and water; continue cooking and stirring, scraping cooked-on juices from bottom and side of pan, until sauce thickens and boils 1 minute. Stir in brown sugar and mustard.
5 Place meat balls in sauce; cover. Simmer 30 minutes.
6 Spread hollows of loaves with butter or margarine; heat in slow oven (325°) 10 minutes.
7 Spoon about 2 cups of the meat balls and sauce into each. Cut into quarters to eat with a knife and fork.

Honolulu Heroes

As American as our 50th state! Filling can be cold cuts and sliced cheeses of your choice, but pile them high

Makes 16 servings

2 loaves Italian bread
  Butter or margarine
3 packages (6 ounces each) sliced cold cuts
1 package (8 ounces) sliced Swiss cheese
1 package (8 ounces) sliced process American cheese
  Boston lettuce
3 medium-size tomatoes, sliced thin
4 hard-cooked eggs, shelled and sliced
1 envelope (2 to a package) onion-soup mix
1 cup (8-ounce carton) dairy sour cream
½ cup milk

1 Split loaves of bread; spread with butter or margarine.
2 Fold half of the cold meat slices and roll remaining; roll Swiss cheese slices; fold American cheese slices. (Cheese rolls perfectly without cracking if warmed to room temperature first.)
3 Layer meat, lettuce, American cheese, tomato slices, egg slices, Swiss cheese, and remaining

(continued)

meat, dividing evenly, onto bottom halves of bread.

4 Blend onion-soup mix with sour cream and milk in a small bowl; spoon part over filling on sandwiches; cover with tops of loaves. Trim with tiny sprigs of parsley held in place with fancy wooden picks. To serve sandwich, cut each into 8 thick slices, serve remaining dressing separately.

Chicken Steamers

They're stacked three layers high with a cool avocado spread and fruited meat salad as the fillings

Makes 16 servings

1 broiler-fryer, weighing about 2½ pounds
1 cup water
1½ teaspoons salt
 Few celery tops
1 can (about 8 ounces) pineapple chunks
½ cup halved green grapes
1 cup mayonnaise or salad dressing
1 medium-size firm ripe avocado
6 slices crisp bacon, crumbled
 Few drops liquid red pepper seasoning
2 loaves Italian bread

1 Combine chicken with water, 1 teaspoon of the salt, and celery tops in a large saucepan; heat to boiling; cover. Simmer 1 hour, or until tender.

2 Remove from broth and cool until easy to handle; strain broth and chill for soup or gravy. Pull skin from chicken and take meat from bones; dice. (There should be about 2 cups.) Place in a medium-size bowl.

3 Drain syrup from pineapple into a cup. Add pineapple and grapes to chicken. Blend 2 tablespoons of the syrup with ½ cup of the mayonnaise or salad dressing and remaining ½ teaspoon salt in a small bowl; fold into chicken mixture. Chill.

4 Halve avocado; pit and peel. Mash in a small bowl; stir in crumbled bacon, ¼ cup of the remaining mayonnaise or salad dressing, and red pepper seasoning. (Fix avocado mixture no longer than an hour ahead so that it keeps its bright color.)

5 Cut each loaf of bread lengthwise into 3 even slices; spread with remaining ¼ cup mayonnaise or salad dressing.

6 Spread avocado mixture on bottom slices and chicken salad on middle slices; stack back in shape; cover with top slices. Cut each sandwich crosswise into 8 thick slices.

Mauna Loa Cream Tower

Big and showy, it calls for three flavors of packaged ice cream and sherbet plus a simple molding trick

Makes 16 servings

1 pint raspberry sherbet
2 pints orange sherbet
½ gallon vanilla ice cream

1 Pack raspberry sherbet into the bottom of a deep 12-cup mold; freeze until firm.

2 Repeat with orange sherbet, then vanilla ice cream; cover. Freeze until serving time.

3 When ready to serve, dip mold *very quickly* in and out of a pan of hot water; invert onto a large serving plate; lift off mold. Frame ice cream with BROWNIE ROUNDS *(recipe follows)* and your choice of sundae sauces.

Hilo Fruits

Pineapple, papaya, and bananas blend with ginger for a different ice-cream topper

Makes 4 cups

1 can (about 14 ounces) pineapple chunks
1 jar (14 ounces) papaya, drained and cubed
2 tablespoons chopped crystallized or preserved ginger
2 medium-size firm ripe bananas

1 Combine pineapple and syrup, papaya, and ginger in a medium-size bowl; chill at least a half hour to season.

2 Just before serving, peel bananas and slice; fold into fruit mixture. Serve in small bowls to spoon over ice cream.

Islands Sundae Sauce

Royally red and lightly spiced! Just see how easily it goes together with frozen punch

Makes 2½ cups

2 cans (6 ounces each) frozen concentrate for juicy red Hawaiian punch
2 cups white corn syrup
½ cup water
1 three-inch piece stick cinnamon

1 Combine concentrate for punch, corn syrup, water, and cinnamon in a large heavy saucepan;

heat slowly, stirring constantly, to boiling, then cook 15 minutes, or until slightly thickened.
2 Remove cinnamon stick. Cool, then chill if made ahead. (For best flavor and easy spooning, remove sauce from refrigerator at least a half hour before serving.) Serve in small bowls to spoon over ice cream.

Kona Cream

This rich sauce owes its candylike flavor to brown sugar and coffee. Recipe makes lots, but it's a good keeper

Makes 4 cups

    1½ cups firmly packed light brown sugar
     2 tablespoons instant coffee powder
       Dash of salt
     1 cup water
     2 cans (about 15 ounces each) sweetened
       condensed milk (not evaporated)
     2 teaspoons rum flavoring or extract

1 Combine brown sugar, instant coffee, salt, and water in a medium-size saucepan.
2 Heat, stirring constantly, to boiling, then cook, without stirring, to 230° on a candy thermometer. (A teaspoon of syrup will spin a thread when dropped from spoon.) Remove from heat.
3 Stir hot syrup into condensed milk in a medium-size bowl; stir in rum flavoring or extract. Chill. Serve in small bowls to spoon over ice cream.

Brownie Rounds

What could be more popular? And it's fun to tint the frosting

Bake at 350° for 10 minutes.
Makes 4 dozen

     1 package (about 1 pound) brownie mix
     2 eggs
     2 tablespoons water
     1 can (1 pound, 5 ounces) vanilla frosting
       Yellow and green food colorings

1 Combine brownie mix, eggs, and water in a medium-size bowl; beat until blended.
2 Drop by teaspoonfuls, 2 inches apart, on greased cookie sheets.
3 Bake in moderate oven (350°) 10 minutes, or until firm. Cool on cookie sheets 1 minute, then remove to wire racks; cool completely.

4 Divide frosting into 2 small bowls; tint one pale yellow and the other green with food colorings. Spread each color on half of the cookies. Sprinkle with decorating sequins and flowers, if you wish.

AT HOME BUFFET FOR 12

Glazed Liver Pâté
Scandinavian Appetizer Tray
Salmon Mousse in Aspic
Fish Balls with Parsley Sauce
Turkey-Ham Galantine
Sweet-Sour Brown Beans
Dilled Potato-Salad Platter
Caraway Cabbage Toss
Assorted Breads and Crackers
Dessert Cheese Tray
Lingonberry Torte
Swedish Apple Cake

Glazed Liver Pâté

Herbs and spices provide a piquant flavor for this pâté

Bake at 350° for 2 hours.
Makes 12 servings.

     2 pounds calf's liver
     ½ pound sliced bacon, cut in 1-inch pieces
     1 medium-size onion, chopped (½ cup)
     1 clove of garlic, sliced
     1 envelope instant chicken broth
     1 bay leaf
     ½ teaspoon ground allspice
     ½ teaspoon leaf thyme, crumbled
     1 cup cream for whipping
     1 can (2 ounces) anchovy fillets
     ¼ cup sifted all-purpose flour
     ¼ teaspoon salt
     ¼ teaspoon pepper
     2 eggs
     2 tablespoons brandy
     1 envelope unflavored gelatin
     1 can (10½ ounces) condensed beef broth
       Carrot, green onion, and pitted ripe olives

1 Two days before your party, bake liver loaf. Grease a loaf pan, 9x5x3; line with double-thick foil, leaving a 3 inch overhang all around.
2 Wash liver; cut into 2-inch pieces. Combine with bacon, onion, garlic, chicken broth, bay leaf, allspice, and thyme in a large frying pan; cover. (Do not add water.) Simmer, stirring several times, 30 minutes; remove bay leaf.

(continued)

3 Pour half of mixture into an electric-blender container; add half of the cream and anchovies with oil; beat until smooth. Pour into a large bowl. Repeat with remaining liver mixture, cream, and anchovies.

4 Stir in flour, salt, and pepper; beat in eggs and brandy. Spoon into prepared pan; fold ends of foil over top.

5 Set pan in a larger pan on oven shelf; pour boiling water into pan to a depth of about 1 inch.

6 Bake in moderate oven (350°) 2 hours. Remove from water; chill overnight.

7 One day before your party, glaze loaf. Sprinkle gelatin over half of the beef broth in a small saucepan; heat, stirring constantly, until gelatin dissolves; remove from heat. Stir in remaining broth; cool.

8 Loosen chilled loaf around edges of pan with a knife; peel back foil and lift loaf from pan; peel off foil.

9 Cut flower, leaf, and stem shapes from carrot, onion, and olives. Wash pan and dry; place in a larger pan of ice and water to speed setting.

10 Pour ½ cup of the gelatin mixture into pan; chill just until sticky-firm. Arrange cutouts in a pretty pattern on sticky-firm gelatin. Carefully spoon in just enough more gelatin mixture to cover vegetables; let set until sticky-firm.

11 Place liver loaf carefully over gelatin in pan; pour in all remaining gelatin mixture. Remove from ice. Chill in refrigerator overnight.

12 When ready to serve, run a sharp-tip thin-blade knife around top of loaf; dip pan *very quickly* in and out of hot water. Cover with a chilled serving plate; turn upside down; lift off pan. Garnish with small crisp lettuce leaves, if you wish. Cut in thin slices; serve with crackers.

Scandinavian Appetizer Tray

The food combination is colorful so select an attractive serving dish

Makes 12 servings.

6 medium-size cucumbers
1½ cups cider vinegar
½ cup water
½ cup sugar
1 teaspoon salt
¼ teaspoon white pepper
6 tablespoons chopped fresh dill
   OR: 1 tablespoon dillweed
2 jars (8 ounces each) herring in wine sauce
2 jars (1 pound each) sliced pickled beets

With a buffet, you can be as formal or as informal as you wish. But do make sure that all the food is in easy reach of your guests, as in this **At Home Buffet for 12.**

1 medium-size onion, peeled, sliced, and separated into rings

1 Pare cucumbers and slice very thin; place in a medium-size bowl.

2 Combine vinegar, water, sugar, salt, and pepper in a small bowl; stir until sugar dissolves. Pour over cucumber slices; sprinkle with dill. Chill at least 2 hours to season.

3 When ready to serve, drain liquids from cucumbers, herring, and beets. Spoon cucumbers into a shallow serving dish; place in the center of a large serving tray. Arrange herring and beets in sections around cucumbers. Garnish beets with onion rings, and cucumbers and herring with sprigs of fresh dill, if you wish.

Salmon Mousse in Aspic

So simple to make—but, oh, so elegant

Makes 12 servings.

2 envelopes unflavored gelatin
2 cans (about 13 ounces each) consommé madrilène
½ cup dry white wine
2 cans (1 pound each) salmon
¼ cup mayonnaise or salad dressing
¼ cup cream for whipping

1 Soften gelatin in 1 can of the madrilène in a medium-size saucepan. Heat, stirring constantly, until gelatin dissolves; remove from heat. Stir in remaining 1 can madrilène.

2 Measure out ½ cup of the mixture and set aside. Stir wine into remaining mixture in saucepan.

3 Drain salmon; bone and flake into a large bowl. Beat in the ½ cup gelatin mixture and mayonnaise or salad dressing. Beat cream until stiff in a small bowl; fold into salmon mixture. Chill while preparing mold.

4 Place a 6-cup fish-shape mold in a large pan of ice and water; let stand 5 minutes; pour in gelatin-wine mixture. Chill 20 minutes, or until gelatin forms a thin coat on bottom and sides of mold; pour off unset gelatin mixture into a bowl.

(continued)

5 Spoon salmon mixture over layer in mold, spreading to within ½ inch of sides of mold; chill until softly set.

6 Spoon remaining gelatin mixture back into mold around salmon and on top; remove mold from ice and water. Chill in refrigerator at least 6 hours, or until firm.

7 When ready to serve, run a sharp-tip thin-blade knife around top of salad; dip mold *very quickly* in and out of hot water. Cover with a chilled serving plate; turn upside down; lift off mold. Garnish with cucumber cups filled with twists of lemon rind and mayonnaise or salad dressing, and chicory or curly endive, if you wish.

Fish Balls with Parsley Sauce

Haddock is the star of this side dish

Makes 12 servings

> 2 packages (1 pound each) frozen haddock fillets
> 1 cup cracker meal (from an about-10-ounce package)
> 2 teaspoons salt
> ¼ teaspoon white pepper
> 1½ cups light cream or table cream
> PARSLEY SAUCE (recipe follows)
> Paprika

1 Thaw haddock just enough to cut into chunks with a heavy knife. Put through a food grinder twice, using a fine blade. Place in a large bowl.

2 Beat in cracker meal, salt, pepper, and cream until mixture is smooth.

3 Moisten hands; shape mixture into 1-inch balls.

4 Half-fill a large frying pan with water; heat to boiling. Drop fish balls, half at a time, into pan; simmer 10 minutes. Lift out with a slotted spoon; drain on paper toweling. Place in a serving dish; keep warm until all are cooked.

5 Pour PARSLEY SAUCE over fish balls; sprinkle with paprika.

PARSLEY SAUCE

Melt 6 tablespoons (¾ stick) butter or margarine in a large saucepan. Stir in ⅓ cup sifted all-purpose flour, 1 teaspoon salt, ⅛ teaspoon nutmeg, and a dash of white pepper; cook, stirring constantly, until bubbly. Stir in 2½ cups light cream or table cream; continue cooking and stirring until sauce thickens and boils 1 minute. Just before serving, stir in ¼ cup chopped parsley.

Turkey-Ham Galantine

Boned and seasoned turkey-ham is served in its own jelly—with a little help from gelatin

Makes 12 servings

> 2 packaged frozen boneless turkey-ham roasts, weighing 2 pounds each
> 2 envelopes unflavored gelatin
> ½ cup light cream or table cream
> 4 tablespoons (½ stick) butter or margarine
> 2 tablespoons all-purpose flour
> ½ teaspoon salt
> 3 cups chicken broth (from two 13¾ ounce cans)
> 2 hard-cooked egg yolks
> Carrot slices
> Parsley sprigs

1 Two days before your party, roast frozen turkey-ham roasts in their foil packages, following label directions. Remove from packages; cool; wrap in foil or transparent wrap; chill.

2 One day before your party, sprinkle 1 envelope of the gelatin over cream in a small bowl; let stand several minutes to soften gelatin.

3 Melt 2 tablespoons of the butter or margarine in a medium-size saucepan; stir in flour, salt, and 1 cup of the chicken broth. Cook, stirring constantly, until mixture thickens and boils 1 minute; stir in gelatin mixture until dissolved; remove from heat. Chill until as thick as unbeaten egg white.

4 Place turkey-ham roasts on a wire rack set in a jelly-roll pan. Spoon part of the thickened gelatin mixture over roasts to coat; chill until set. Repeat twice more with remaining gelatin mixture, chilling until set between each coat, to make a smooth even coating over roasts.

5 Press egg yolks through a sieve into a small bowl; blend in remaining 2 tablespoons butter or margarine. Press mixture through a cake-decorating set onto top of one roast to form blossoms. Cut petal shapes from carrot slices and arrange with sprigs of parsley around eggs to make flowers and stems.

6 Sprinkle remaining 1 envelope gelatin over remaining 2 cups chicken broth in a small saucepan; heat, stirring constantly, until gelatin dissolves. Chill until as thick as unbeaten egg white. Spoon part over decorations on roast to coat well. Remove both roasts to a clean tray or plate; chill.

7 Pour remaining gelatin mixture into a pan, 8x8x2; chill several hours, or until firm.

8 When ready to serve, place decorated roast on a large serving plate; slice second roast and arrange slices at side. Cut gelatin mixture in pan into very tiny cubes; spoon evenly around meat on plate.

Sweet-Sour Brown Beans

A zesty side dish rich in protein

Makes 12 servings.

 2 pounds dried Swedish brown beans
10 cups water
 3 teaspoons salt
½ cup firmly packed brown sugar
½ cup cider vinegar
  Sliced green onions

1 Wash beans and sort; combine with water in a kettle.

2 Heat to boiling; cook 2 minutes; cover. Remove from heat; let stand 1 hour.

3 Stir in salt and just enough water, if needed, to cover beans. Heat to boiling; simmer 1½ hours, or until beans are tender. (If needed during cooking, add additional water.)

4 Stir in brown sugar and vinegar; heat 10 minutes to blend flavors. Spoon into a heated serving bowl; sprinkle with sliced green onions.

Note: If you cannot find Swedish brown beans in your supermarket, substitute dried red kidney beans.

Dilled Potato-Salad Platter

Pepper and dill provide the flavor accents

Makes 12 servings.

5 pounds medium-size potatoes
2 cups chopped celery
1 medium-size onion, chopped (½ cup)
2 cups mayonnaise or salad dressing
½ cup milk
2 tablespoons dill seeds, crushed
1 teaspoon salt
  Dash of pepper
  Boston lettuce
  STUFFED EGGS (recipe follows)
1 tablespoon chopped parsley

1 Cook potatoes, covered, in boiling salted water in a large saucepan 45 minutes, or just until tender; drain. Cool until easy to handle, then cube and combine with celery and onion in a large bowl.

2 Blend mayonnaise or salad dressing, milk, dill seeds, salt, and pepper in a small bowl; fold into potato mixture.

3 Spoon into a 12-cup bowl; press down lightly with back of spoon to make top even; cover. Chill several hours.

4 When ready to serve, loosen salad around edge with a thin-blade knife; invert onto a serving plate; lift off bowl. Frame salad with lettuce; arrange STUFFED EGGS around edge. Sprinkle salad with parsley and garnish with shredded green-onion tops, if you wish.

STUFFED EGGS
Hard-cook 12 eggs; shell. Cut each in half lengthwise; scoop out yolks into a medium-size

(continued)

bowl; mash well. Stir in ½ cup mayonnaise or salad dressing and 1 tablespoon prepared mustard. Pile back into whites. Top each with red caviar (from a 4-ounce jar).

Caraway Cabbage Toss

Choose a cabbage with trim leaves and good color

Makes 12 servings

1 medium-size head cabbage
⅔ cup vegetable oil
⅓ cup vinegar
1 tablespoon caraway seeds
1 teaspoon sugar
½ teaspoon salt
  Dash of pepper
3 medium-size apples
  Large romaine leaves

1 Trim outer leaves from cabbage; quarter head and cut out core. Shred cabbage fine. (There will be about 9 cups.) Place in a large bowl.
2 Combine vegetable oil, vinegar, caraway seeds, sugar, salt, and pepper in a jar with a tight-fitting lid; shake well to mix. Pour over cabbage; toss lightly; cover. Chill several hours.
3 When ready to serve, quarter apples; core; slice thin crosswise. Set aside a few slices for garnish; toss remainder with cabbage mixture. Spoon into a romaine-lined salad bowl; overlap remaining apple slices on top.

Lingonberry Torte

A super dessert rounds out the buffet

Bake at 350° for 10 minutes,
then at 325° for 30 minutes.
Makes one 9-inch 2-layer torte.

3 squares unsweetened chocolate
1 cup milk
1 cup sifted all-purpose flour
2½ teaspoons baking powder
½ teaspoon salt
4 whole eggs
1 egg yolk
1⅓ cups sugar
1½ teaspoons almond extract
  LINGONBERRY JAM (recipe follows)
  COFFEE FROSTING (recipe follows)

1 Melt chocolate in milk in top of a double boiler over hot water; remove from heat; cool.
2 Sift flour, baking powder, and salt onto wax paper.
3 Beat egg and egg yolk until fluffy-light in a medium-size bowl; slowly beat in sugar until creamy-thick. Stir in almond extract and chocolate mixture; fold in flour mixture. Pour into 2 greased 9x1½-inch layer-cake pans, dividing evenly.
4 Bake in moderate oven (350°) 10 minutes. Lower oven temperature to slow (325°). Bake 30 minutes longer, or until a wooden pick inserted in center comes out clean.
5 Cool layers in pans on wire racks 5 minutes. Loosen around edges with a knife; turn out; cool completely.
6 Spread LINGONBERRY JAM over one layer; place on a serving plate; top with second layer. Frost side and top of torte with COFFEE FROSTING, spreading evenly.

LINGONBERRY JAM
Combine 1 jar (about 15 ounces) lingonberries with ½ cup sugar in a small saucepan. Heat, stirring constantly, to boiling, then cook, stirring constantly, about 5 minutes, or until mixture is very thick. Cool.

COFFEE FROSTING
Sift 1 package (1 pound) 10X (confectioners' powdered) sugar onto wax paper. Cream ½ cup (1 stick) butter or margarine with half of the sugar until fluffy-light in a medium-size bowl. Combine 1 tablespoon instant coffee, 1 teaspoon vanilla, and 3 tablespoons milk in a cup; slowly beat into butter mixture, adding alternately with remaining sugar, until frosting is smooth and easy to spread. Makes enough to frost two 9-inch layers.

Swedish Apple Cake

An apple cake with a crushed zwieback crust

Bake at 350° for 30 minutes.
Makes 12 servings.

1 package (6 ounces) zwieback
½ cup (1 stick) butter or margarine, melted
2 teaspoons grated lemon rind
2 jars or cans (15 or 16 ounces each) applesauce
1 package (about 3 ounces) vanilla pudding and pie filling mix
3 cups milk
2 teaspoons vanilla
1 cup cream for whipping

1 Crush zwieback fine. (There will be about 2½ cups.) Toss with melted butter or margarine in a large bowl. Measure out 1 cup of the mixture and press into a baking dish, 9x9x2.
2 Stir lemon rind into applesauce in a medium-size bowl; spread half over crumb layer in pan. Sprinkle with half of the remaining crumb mixture; spread with remaining applesauce mixture; sprinkle with remaining crumb mixture.
3 Bake in moderate oven (350°) 30 minutes, or until firm and golden. Cool in dish on wire rack.
4 Several hours before serving, prepare pudding mix with milk, following label directions; stir in vanilla; chill.
5 Just before serving, beat cream until stiff in a medium-size bowl. Cut cake into squares; place on rimmed serving plates. Spoon custard sauce around cake; top with whipped cream. Garnish each with a small spoonful of red currant jelly, if you wish.

MADE-EASY HAM BUFFET FOR 25

Buffet Glazed Ham
Sweet-Sour Mustard Cream
Button Biscuits
Meat Ball Miniatures
Dilled Relish Tray
Pâté-Cheese Mold
Crisp Crackers
Candlelight Cake
Holiday Punch

Buffet Glazed Ham

This no-carve baked ham boasts a handsome fruit glaze and a Della Robbia crown

Bake at 325° for 2 hours and 30 minutes

For 25 generous servings, plus some for a bonus dish or two, buy an about-10-pound canned boneless ready-to-eat ham. Ask your meatman to slice it into ¼-inch-thick slices, keeping it in its original shape, then tie securely with string. (During slow shopping hours he will be glad to do this.) When ready to heat, place ham in a large shallow baking pan. Bake in slow oven (325°) 2 hours; spread part of the CURRANT GLAZE (recipe follows) over top. Continue baking, basting with more glaze, 30 minutes longer, or until ham is richly glazed. Place on a heated serving platter or tray; cut away strings. Garnish

top of ham with a crown of marzipan fruits and halved pecans, and frame with watercress, as pictured.

CURRANT GLAZE
Combine 1 cup currant jelly with 2 tablespoons lemon juice and ½ teaspoon pumpkin-pie spice in a small saucepan. Heat, stirring constantly, just until well-blended. Makes about 1 cup.

Sweet-Sour Mustard Cream

Spread this zippy-seasoned sauce on the ham, and pop into a tiny biscuit

Makes about 1 cup

2 tablespoons butter or margarine
2 tablespoons all-purpose flour
2 tablespoons dry mustard
1 tablespoon sugar
1 teaspoon salt
　Dash of cayenne
1 cup milk
1 egg, beaten
2 tablespoons cider vinegar

1 Melt butter or margarine in a medium-size saucepan; stir in flour, mustard, sugar, salt, and cayenne. Cook, stirring constantly, just until bubbly. Stir in milk; continue cooking and stirring until sauce thickens and boils 1 minute.
2 Stir ½ cup of the hot mixture into beaten egg in a small bowl, then stir back into remaining sauce in pan; cook, stirring constantly, 1 minute longer. Remove from heat; stir in vinegar.
3 Cool, then chill. Just before serving, beat until smooth.

Button Biscuits

Bake these dainty biscuits, part at a time, to keep them coming piping hot

Bake at 450° for 12 minutes.
Makes 4 dozen

4 cups sifted all-purpose flour
6 tablespoons baking powder
2 teaspoons sugar
1 teaspoon salt
½ cup vegetable shortening
1½ cups milk

1 Sift flour, baking powder, sugar, and salt into a large bowl; cut in shortening with a pastry blender until mixture is crumbly; stir in milk to make a soft dough.

(continued)

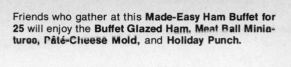

Friends who gather at this **Made-Easy Ham Buffet for 25** will enjoy the **Buffet Glazed Ham, Meat Ball Miniatures, Pâté-Cheese Mold,** and **Holiday Punch.**

2 Turn out onto a lightly floured pastry cloth or board; knead gently ½ minute. Roll out to a rectangle ½ inch thick; cut into rounds with a 1½-inch cutter; place on greased cookie sheets. Reroll and cut out all trimmings.
3 Bake in very hot oven (450°) 12 minutes, or until golden.

Meat Ball Miniatures

Flavorful beef and mild veal go into these titbits to serve in a gingery sauce

Makes 25 servings

2 *pounds ground beef*
2 *pounds ground veal*
½ *cup sifted all-purpose flour*
½ *teaspoon ground ginger*
1 *cup light cream or table cream*
¼ *cup soy sauce*
4 *tablespoons (½ stick) butter or margarine*
  GINGER SOY SAUCE *(recipe follows)*
2 *medium-size green peppers*
1 *can (5 ounces) water chestnuts*

1 Combine ground beef and veal, flour, and ginger in the large bowl of an electric mixer; beat until blended, then beat in cream and soy sauce, 1 tablespoon at a time, until mixture is smooth and pastelike.
2 Shape into tiny balls. (This amount will make as many as 180 marble-size balls. Shaping can be done ahead and balls chilled until ready to cook.)
3 Sauté meat balls, a single layer at a time, in part of the butter or margarine until cooked through in a large frying pan. Keep hot while cooking remaining meat balls, adding remaining butter or margarine as needed, and making GINGER SOY SAUCE.
4 Quarter green peppers; remove seeds; cut peppers in small squares. Drain water chestnuts; cut in thin slices.
5 Pour GINGER SOY SAUCE into a chafing dish or keep-hot server. Spoon meat balls on top, basting with sauce; tuck in green peppers and water chestnuts. Serve with wooden picks for spearing meat balls.
  GINGER SOY SAUCE—After all meat balls are cooked, tip pan so fat will rise to top; pour off

(continued)

all fat, leaving brown drippings in pan. Measure ¼ cup fat and return to pan; blend in ¼ cup flour and ¼ teaspoon ground ginger; cook, stirring constantly, just until bubbly. Stir in 2 cups water and 3 tablespoons soy sauce; continue cooking and stirring, scraping cooked-on bits from bottom and side of pan, until sauce thickens and boils 1 minute. Makes about 2 cups.

Dilled Relish Tray

Such a good keeper that it can be made days ahead

Makes 25 servings

2 large Bermuda onions
4 medium-size cucumbers
2 cans (3 or 4 ounces each) mushroom caps
1¾ cups sugar
4 teaspoons salt
2 teaspoons dillweed
2 cups white vinegar
1 cup water

1 Peel onions; slice thin and separate into rings; place in a large bowl. Pare cucumbers and score with a fork; slice cucumbers thin; place in a medium-size bowl. Drain liquid from mushrooms and save for soup or gravy; place mushrooms in a small bowl.
2 Combine sugar, salt, dillweed, vinegar, and water in a medium-size saucepan; heat to boiling. Pour over vegetables in each bowl; cover. Chill several hours or overnight.
3 When ready to serve, remove vegetables from liquid with a slotted spoon. Pile into a sectioned relish tray or into separate small bowls.

Pâté-Cheese Mold

A stuffed-olive crown sparkles atop this holiday meat-cheese pleaser

Makes 25 servings

MEAT LAYER

1 envelope unflavored gelatin
1 envelope instant chicken broth
   OR: 1 chicken-bouillon cube
1 cup water
1 tablespoon lemon juice
3 large stuffed green olives, sliced
½ pound bologna
¼ cup mayonnaise or salad dressing
¼ cup sweet-mustard relish (from a 9-ounce jar)

CHEESE LAYER

1 envelope unflavored gelatin
¼ cup water
2 wedges (1⅓ ounces each) Camembert cheese
¼ pound blue cheese
¼ teaspoon curry powder
1 egg separated
1 cup (8-ounce carton) dairy sour cream
   Green food coloring

1 Make meat layer: Soften gelatin with chicken broth or bouillon cube in water in a small saucepan. Heat, stirring constantly and crushing cube, if using, with a spoon, just until gelatin dissolves. Measure ¼ cup into a 6-cup mold; stir in lemon juice. (Keep remaining gelatin mixture at room temperature.)
2 Set mold in a pan of ice and water to speed setting; chill just until syrupy-thick. Arrange stuffed-olive slices in gelatin to make a pretty pattern. Chill until sticky-firm.
3 While mold chills, remove skin from bologna; put meat through a food chopper, using a fine blade. Mix with remaining gelatin mixture, mayonnaise or salad dressing, and relish in a medium-size bowl; spoon over sticky-firm olive layer in mold. Continue chilling in same pan of ice and water until sticky-firm while making cheese layer.
4 Make cheese layer: Soften gelatin in water in a small saucepan; heat slowly just until gelatin dissolves.
5 Beat Camembert and blue cheeses until well blended in a medium-size bowl; beat in curry powder, egg yolk, and dissolved gelatin.
6 Beat egg white until it stands in firm peaks in a small bowl. Fold into cheese mixture, then fold in sour cream. Tint mixture light green with a drop or two of food coloring.
7 Spoon over sticky-firm meat layer in mold; cover with wax paper, foil, or transparent wrap. Chill in refrigerator several hours, or until firm. (Overnight is best.)
8 When ready to unmold, run a sharp-tip, thin-blade knife around top of mold, then dip mold *very quickly* in and out of a pan of hot water. Cover mold with a serving plate; turn upside down; gently lift off mold. Surround with your choice of crisp crackers.

Candlelight Cake

Fluffy whipped cream baked right in the cake adds extra moistness. For a festive touch, stand a lighted candle in the center hole

Bake at 325° for 1 hour and 15 minutes.
Makes one 10-inch tube cake

2¾ cups sifted cake flour
 4 teaspoons baking powder
 1 teaspoon salt
 4 eggs, separated
1¾ cups sugar
 1 cup cream for whipping
 1 teaspoon vanilla
 1 teaspoon almond extract
 ⅔ cup milk
  10X (confectioners' powdered) sugar

1 Measure cake flour, baking powder, and salt into a sifter.
2 Beat egg whites until foamy-light and double in volume in a medium-size bowl; beat in ½ cup of the sugar, 1 tablespoon at a time, beating all the time until meringue forms soft peaks. (Set remaining 1¼ cups sugar aside for Step 4.)
3 Beat cream until stiff in a medium-size bowl; chill.
4 Beat egg yolks until creamy-thick in a large bowl; beat in remaining 1¼ cups sugar, 1 tablespoon at a time, beating all the time until mixture is fluffy-light. Beat in vanilla and almond extract.
5 Sift in flour mixture, adding alternately with milk and stirring just until well-blended; fold in meringue and whipped cream until no streaks of white remain. Pour into a greased and floured 10-cup fancy tube mold or a 10-inch angel-cake pan.
6 Bake in slow oven (325°) 1 hour and 15 minutes, or until top springs back when lightly pressed with fingertip.
7 Cool in pan on a wire rack 15 minutes; loosen around edge and tube with a knife, then invert onto a serving plate.
8 When ready to serve, dust lightly with 10X sugar and top with a ring of sliced pistachio nuts, if you wish. Cut into 1-inch-thick wedges.

Holiday Punch

Its cool green color adds a festive note to your party table

Makes 50 punch-cup servings

1 cup sugar
1 two-inch piece of stick cinnamon

5 whole cloves
5 whole allspice
2 cups water
2 cans (6 ounces each) frozen concentrate for lemonade
2 cans (6 ounces each) frozen concentrate for limeade
2 bottles (1 pint, 12 ounces each) quinine water, chilled
2 bottles (1 pint, 12 ounces each) carbonated water, chilled
  ICE BLOCK (directions follow)

1 Combine sugar, cinnamon stick, cloves, allspice, and water in a small saucepan; heat to boiling; simmer 5 minutes. Strain into a medium-size bowl; cool.
2 When ready to mix punch, pour spiced-water mixture into a punch bowl; stir in frozen lemonade and limeade, and quinine and carbonated waters.
3 Float ice block on top. Surround bowl with clusters of green grapes, as pictured, if you wish.

ICE BLOCK
The day before the party, fill a fancy mold that will fit into the punch bowl with water; freeze. To unmold, dip quickly in and out of a pan of hot water; float on top of punch. Garnish with a ring of alternating slices of lemon and lime.

BEEF BUFFET FOR 25

Herbed Beef Roast with Chutney
Fruit Sauce and Mustard Cream
Parker House Midgets
Molded Cheese Pineapple
Seafood Salad Soufflé
Appetizer Vegetables
Tiny Tim Pecan Tarts with fresh and candied fruits and nuts
Strawberry Fruit-Cup Punch

Herbed Beef Roast

Carve this favorite into small thin slices to top with a zippy spread and pop into a tiny oven-warm bun

Roast at 325° for 2¼ hours.
Makes 25 servings

1 beef eye-round roast, weighing from 5 to 6 pounds

(continued)

½ cup sifted all-purpose flour
3 teaspoons salt
1 teaspoon paprika
1 teaspoon leaf basil, crumbled
1 teaspoon leaf marjoram, crumbled
  Watercress

1 Place roast on a sheet of wax paper. Mix remaining ingredients, except watercress, in a cup; pat well into roast. Place on a rack in a shallow baking pan. If using a meat thermometer, insert bulb into thickest part of roast. Do not add water or cover pan.
2 Roast in slow oven (325°) 2¼ hours, or until thermometer registers 140° for rare. Cover pan loosely with foil; let stand at room temperature until serving time.
3 Carve about one third of the roast into very thin slices; cut each slice in three or four pieces. Arrange pieces, along with remaining roast, on a serving platter. Garnish platter with watercress and top roast with a bouquet of radish roses, if you wish. Serve with MUSTARD CREAM and CHUTNEY FRUIT SAUCE (both recipes follow).
Hostess Note: Roast tastes equally inviting served cold, so cook it the day before or morning of your party, if you wish.

Chutney Fruit Sauce

Canned peaches blend with onion and zippy spices for this savory meat spread

Makes 2 cups

1 can (1 pound, 13 ounces) cling-peach slices
1 small onion, chopped (¼ cup)
¼ teaspoon ground cumin
⅛ teaspoon ground allspice
½ teaspoon Worcestershire sauce
¼ teaspoon liquid red pepper seasoning
2 tablespoons lemon juice

1 Drain syrup from peaches into a cup. Measure 2 tablespoonfuls and combine with peaches, onion, cumin, allspice, Worcestershire sauce, and red pepper seasoning in an electric-blender container; cover. Beat at high speed 1 minute, or until smooth; pour into a small saucepan.
2 Heat to boiling, then simmer, stirring often, 5 minutes to blend flavors; remove from heat.
3 Stir in lemon juice; chill.
Hostess Note: If you do not have a blender, place peaches in a small deep bowl and beat with an electric beater until smooth. Mince onion, then combine with peaches and remaining ingredients. Sauce may not be quite so smooth, but it will taste just as good. Another

tip: Although sauce may be made ahead, it tastes best slightly warm, so remove it from refrigerator and let stand at room temperature for an hour before serving.

Mustard Cream

Flavor is delicate and just spicy enough for succulent roast beef

Makes about 2 cups

1 cup mayonnaise or salad dressing
½ cup prepared mustard
½ cup canned condensed beef consommé
¼ cup light cream or table cream

Combine all ingredients in a medium-size bowl; beat with an electric or rotary beater until well blended. Chill.
Hostess Note: Sauce keeps well, so make it a day ahead and store, covered, in the refrigerator.

Parker House Midgets

Each of these buttery gems is just the right size to make into a two-bite sandwich

Bake at 450° for 15 minutes.
Makes 80 tiny rolls

½ cup (1 stick) butter or margarine
4 packages refrigerated plain or buttermilk biscuits

1 Melt butter or margarine in a jelly-roll pan, 15x10x1, while oven heats.
2 Separate the 10 biscuits in each package; cut each in half. (Scissors make the job go fast.) Roll each half into a tiny ball, then flatten with a glass to a 2-inch round; fold round in half.
3 Roll in melted butter or margarine in pan to coat all over, then arrange in a single layer in same pan. (So rolls keep a trim neat shape, arrange in 10 rows of eight each.)
4 Bake in very hot oven (450°) 15 minutes, or until golden. Serve hot.
Hostess note: Rolls may be baked ahead, if you wish, then reheated just before serving time.

Molded Cheese Pineapple

Such a conversation piece! And it's so worth the splurge on a fresh pineapple to get the stately crown

Makes 25 servings

1½ pounds sharp Cheddar cheese, grated (6 cups)
½ pound Swiss cheese, grated (2 cups)
1 package (8 ounces) cream cheese, softened
¼ pound blue cheese, crumbled
½ cup (1 stick) butter or margarine, softened
½ cup apple juice
2 tablespoons lemon juice
1 tablespoon Worcestershire sauce
Whole cloves
Paprika
1 leafy crown from a large fresh pineapple

1 Combine Cheddar, Swiss, cream, and blue cheeses with butter or margarine in the large bowl of an electric mixer. Slowly beat in apple and lemon juices, and Worcestershire sauce; continue beating, scraping down side of bowl often, 5 minutes, or until well blended; cover. Chill several hours, or until firm enough to handle.

2 Shape cheese mixture with your hands into a "pineapple" on a plate; smooth top flat; cover with foil, transparent wrap, or wax paper. Chill several hours, or until very firm.

3 Before serving, mark cheese all over with the tip of a teaspoon to resemble a pineapple; center each mark with a whole clove; lightly sprinkle cheese with paprika. Lift mold onto a serving plate with a pancake turner.

4 Place pineapple crown on top of mold; hold in place with several wooden picks, if needed. Frame with party-size pumpernickel and your favorite crisp crackers, if you wish.

Hostess Note: If there's any cheese left, remove pineapple crown and discard. Cover cheese well and keep chilled. It will stay fresh-tasting for a week or more.

With any buffet for a large number of people, choose a large piece of meat to cut down the work. And there are few better than **Herbed Beef Roast.**

Seafood Salad Soufflé

No need to serve extra dressing with this beauty, for it's molded into both layers

Makes 25 servings

LIME LAYER

1 package (3 ounces) lime-flavor gelatin
1 cup hot water
1 cup (8-ounce carton) dairy sour cream
½ cup mayonnaise or salad dressing
2 tablespoons lemon juice
½ teaspoon salt
   Few drops liquid red pepper seasoning
1 large cucumber

SEAFOOD LAYER

2 envelopes unflavored gelatin
1½ cups water
2 cans (1 pound each) salmon
1 can (about 7 ounces) crabmeat
½ cup mayonnaise or salad dressing
2 tablespoons lemon juice
1 teaspoon salt
¼ teaspoon freshly ground pepper
2 egg whites
1 cup cream for whipping
   Red food coloring

1 Make lime layer: Dissolve lime-flavor gelatin in hot water in a medium-size bowl; stir in sour cream, mayonnaise or salad dressing, lemon juice, salt, and red pepper seasoning. Chill 30 minutes, or until as thick as unbeaten egg white.
2 Cut about 12 thin even slices from cucumber, then trim a sliver from each so it will stand flat around edge of mold; set aside for Step 8. Pare remaining cucumber and trimmings and chop fine; fold into thickened lime-gelatin mixture; pour into a 12-cup fancy tube mold. Chill 30 minutes, or just until sticky-firm.
3 While mixture in mold chills, make seafood layer: Soften gelatin in ½ cup of the water in a small saucepan; heat, stirring constantly, until gelatin dissolves; remove from heat. Stir in remaining 1 cup water.
4 Drain both cans of salmon; bone and flake into a medium-size bowl. Drain crab meat; flake and remove bony tissue, if any; add to salmon.
5 Combine ⅓ each of the seafood and gelatin mixtures at a time in an electric-blender container; cover. Beat at high speed until smooth; pour into a large bowl. Stir in mayonnaise or salad dressing, lemon juice, salt, and pepper.
6 Beat egg whites until they stand in firm peaks in a small bowl. Beat cream until stiff in a medium-size bowl. Fold beaten egg whites, then whipped cream into seafood mixture. Tint salmon color with a few drops food coloring.

Carefully spoon over sticky-firm layer in mold. Chill several hours, or until firm. (Overnight is best.)
7 When ready to serve, run a sharp-tip, thin-blade knife around top of salad, then dip mold *very quickly* in and out of a pan of hot water. Cover mold with a serving plate; turn upside down; gently lift off mold.
8 Stand saved cucumber slices, flat edge down, around side of salad. Fill center with a few crisp romaine or curly endive leaves, if you wish.

Appetizer Vegetables

Tart lemon butter turns crisply cooked vegetables into a delightfully different titbit.

Makes 25 servings

1 bunch broccoli (about 2 pounds)
1 medium-size cauliflower
2 packages (9 ounces each) frozen artichoke hearts
2 tablespoons finely chopped onion
½ cup (1 stick) butter or margarine
¼ teaspoon salt
¼ teaspoon paprika
3 tablespoons lemon juice
   Diced pimiento

1 Cut broccoli flowerets from stems, saving stems to cook for another meal; halve large flowerets. Trim green leafy stems from cauliflower; break cauliflower into flowerets; halve any large ones.
2 Cook both vegetables, covered, in boiling salted water in separate large saucepans 8 minutes, or just until crisply tender; drain. Cook artichoke hearts, following label directions; drain. Keep all hot.
3 Sauté onion in butter or margarine in a small frying pan 2 minutes; remove from heat. Stir in salt, paprika, and lemon juice.
4 When ready to serve, arrange artichoke hearts at either end of a large chafing dish or keep-hot server; arrange broccoli and cauliflowerets in center. Drizzle lemon butter over all. Sprinkle artichoke hearts with pimiento.

Tiny Tim Pecan Tarts

Filling is similar to pecan pie—and just sweet enough for a light party top-off

Bake at 375° for 20 minutes.
Makes 3 dozen

1 package piecrust mix
3 eggs
¾ cup sugar
¼ teaspoon salt
1 cup dark corn syrup
1 teaspoon vanilla
3 tablespoons all-purpose flour
1 cup cream for whipping
  Pecan halves

1 Prepare piecrust mix, following label directions, or make pastry from your favorite double-crust recipe. Roll out, half at a time, to a rectangle, 14x10, on a lightly floured pastry cloth or board. Cut out 12 rounds with a 3-inch plain or scalloped cutter.
2 Fit each round into a tiny muffin-pan cup, pressing firmly against bottom and side. Repeat with remaining half of dough; reroll trimmings and cut out to make 36 shells in all.
3 Beat eggs slightly in a medium-size bowl; stir in sugar, salt, corn syrup, and vanilla, then flour. Spoon about 1 tablespoonful into each shell.
4 Bake in moderate oven (375°) 20 minutes, or until pastry is golden and filling is set. Cool in pans on wire racks 10 minutes, then remove carefully; cool completely.
5 Just before serving, beat cream until stiff in a small bowl. Spoon a dollop on top of each tart; decorate each with a pecan half.

Hostess Note: Parts may be baked the day before your party, if you wish. Place in a single layer in a jelly-roll pan or on a cookie sheet and cover with transparent wrap or wax paper. Store in a cool dry place.

Strawberry Fruit-Cup Punch

It looks so inviting on your party table. Flavor is slightly sweet yet tangy

Makes 25 servings, about 1 cup each

9 packages (10 ounces each) frozen sliced strawberries, partly thawed
¾ cup currant jelly
¾ cup lime juice
6 cups finely crushed ice
6 cups water
1 large lime, sliced thin

1 Combine 3 packages of the strawberries, ¼ cup of the currant jelly, and ¼ cup of the lime juice in an electric-blender container; cover. Beat until smooth; pour into a large punch bowl. Repeat two more times with remaining berries, jelly, and lime juice.
2 Stir in ice and water until well blended. Float lime slices on top. Serve in punch cups or dainty glasses.
Hostess Note: If your punch bowl is small, mix punch, one third at a time, and refill bowl as needed.

BRIDAL BUFFET

Crab-Shrimp Imperial
Buffet Mousse Ring
Cranberry Crown
Buttered Green and Wax Beans
Buttercup Biscuits
Ripe and Green Olives
Preserved Mixed Fruits
Bridal Cake   Coffee

Crab-Shrimp Imperial

Succulent seafood and rice bake in the richest, creamiest sauce

Bake at 350° for 45 minutes.
Makes 16 servings, ¾ cup each

1½ cups uncooked regular rice
2 vegetable-bouillon cubes
2 cups hot water
2 tablespoons chopped parsley
2 cans (10¾ ounces each) condensed cream of shrimp soup
1¼ cups milk
2 teaspoons lemon juice
⅛ teaspoon ground nutmeg
2 packages (about 6 ounces each) frozen, thawed king crabmeat
1½ pounds fresh or frozen raw shrimps, cooked and deveined
1 can (6 ounces) sliced mushrooms
1 cup soft bread crumbs (2 slices)
¼ cup toasted slivered almonds (from a 5-ounce can)
2 tablespoons butter or margarine, melted

1 Cook rice just until tender in large saucepan, following label directions. (Rice should be fluffy-dry.)

(continued)

2 Dissolve bouillon cubes in hot water in a 2-cup measure; pour over rice. Stir in parsley; set aside for Step 5.

3 While rice cooks, combine soup and milk in top of large double boiler; heat, stirring once or twice, over simmering water until well blended and bubbly-hot. Stir in lemon juice and nutmeg; remove from heat.

4 Drain and pick over crabmeat, leaving meat in chunks and carefully removing any bony tissue. Set 2 or 3 chunks, along with 2 or 3 shrimps, aside for garnish in Step 7. Fold remaining crab and shrimps, plus mushrooms and liquid, into sauce.

5 Spoon about ⅓ into a buttered 12-cup baking dish; top with half of the rice. Make another layer of each, using half of remaining crab-shrimp sauce and all of the rice. Spoon remaining sauce over.

6 Toss bread crumbs and almonds with melted butter or margarine in small saucepan; spoon around edge of baking dish.

7 Bake in moderate oven (350°) 45 minutes, or until sauce bubbles around edge and crumbs are golden-brown. Pile saved crabmeat and shrimps in center.

Tips for the hostess: This is a perfect make-ahead to keep chilled or even to freeze. If chilled, take from refrigerator; remove cover, and place in a cold oven; set temperature and bake until bubbly-hot. To freeze: Make in a freezer-to-oven casserole, cool, cover or wrap in foil or transparent wrap and freeze. Take from freezer 2 hours ahead of your party and let start to thaw in the refrigerator, then place in a cold oven and bake until bubbly.

Buffet Mousse Ring

Lots of chicken and ham, tangy pineapple and crisp water chestnuts go into this rich soufflélike salad mold

Makes 16 servings, ½ cup each

2 *large whole chicken breasts (about 2 pounds)*
2 *cups water*
1 *small onion, sliced*
   Handful of celery tops
1 *teaspoon salt*
1 *bay leaf*
4 *peppercorns*
1 *can (about 8 ounces) pineapple chunks*
2 *envelopes unflavored gelatin*
1 *tablespoon lemon juice*
3 *drops liquid red pepper seasoning*
1 *cup mayonnaise or salad dressing*

1 *teaspoon prepared mustard*
½ *pound cooked ham*
1 *can (5 ounces) water chestnuts, drained*

1 Combine chicken breasts, water, onion, celery tops, salt, bay leaf and peppercorns in a large saucepan; simmer, covered, 30 minutes, or until chicken is tender.

2 While chicken cooks, drain syrup from pineapple into a 1-cup measure; add water, if needed, to make ½ cup. Stir in gelatin to soften. Set pineapple aside for Steps 8 and 9.

3 Remove chicken from broth; strain broth into a 4-cup measure; add water, if needed, to make 3 cups. Return to same saucepan; stir in softened gelatin.

4 Heat slowly, stirring constantly, until gelatin dissolves; remove from heat. Stir in lemon juice and red pepper seasoning. Measure out ½ cup and set aside for making topping in Step 8. Cool remaining gelatin-mixture in saucepan for Step 6.

5 Slip skin from chicken; remove meat from bones, then dice into small cubes. (There should be about 1½ cups.) Place in a medium-size bowl.

6 Blend mayonnaise or salad dressing and mustard into gelatin in saucepan. Pour into an ice-cube tray; freeze 20 minutes, or just until firm about 1 inch in from edges.

7 To make the fancy top on mold, set aside enough ham to make twelve 2-inch-long strips, each ¼ inch thick. Otherwise dice all of ham. (There should be about 1½ cups.) Slice water chestnuts very thin. Add chestnuts and diced ham to chicken in bowl.

8 Place an 8-cup ring mold in a bowl or pan partly filled with ice cubes and water to speed chilling. If making a plain top, pour the ½ cup saved gelatin into mold; chill until sticky-firm.

To make the fancy top, pour ¼ cup of the saved gelatin into mold; chill until mixture is as thick as unbeaten egg white. Arrange some of the chicken, ham strips, pineapple chunks and water chestnut slices in an attractive pattern in gelatin. Spoon remaining ¼ cup gelatin over; chill until sticky firm.

9 Spoon partly frozen gelatin mixture into a chilled large bowl; beat until thick and fluffy; fold in remaining chicken, ham, pineapple and water chestnuts. Spoon over sticky-firm gelatin layer in mold. Chill several hours, or overnight.

10 To unmold, run a sharp-tip, thin-blade knife around top of mold, then dip *very quickly* in and out of a pan of hot water. Moisten a small cookie sheet with cold water. (This will keep mold from sticking and make it easy to slide onto serving tray later.) Cover mold with cookie sheet; turn upside down, then gently lift off mold. Chill until serving time.

11 Slide mold from cookie sheet onto a flat serving tray, lifting and pushing mold at the same time with a spatula moistened with water. Fill center of ring with salad greens, if you wish.

Tips for the hostess: Don't hesitate to make this mold a day or even two ahead, as it will hold well in the refrigerator. Unmold about an hour before serving to avoid last-minute fussing. This ring, as well as the CRANBERRY CROWN, should be served on a large flat tray or platter.

Cranberry Crown

It looks so pretty on a party table. The berries literally shine through the shimmering gelatin

Makes 16 servings, ½ cup each

3 packages (3 ounces each) orange-flavor
   gelatin
2 cups hot water
1 can (1 pound) whole-fruit cranberry sauce
 1 cup bottled cranberry-juice cocktail
 1 bottle (7 ounces) ginger ale
 1 cup chopped celery
½ cup chopped sweet pickles
¼ cup sweet-pickle juice
   Mayonnaise or salad dressing

1 Dissolve gelatin in hot water in large bowl. Break up cranberry sauce in can with a fork; stir into gelatin mixture with cranberry-juice cocktail and ginger ale. Chill until mixture is as thick as unbeaten egg white.
2 Stir in celery, pickles and juice; spoon into an 8-cup ring mold. Chill several hours, or until firm.
3 To unmold, run a sharp-tip, thin-blade knife around top of mold, then dip *very quickly* in and out of a pan of hot water. Moisten a small cookie sheet with cold water. (This will keep mold from sticking and make it easy to slide onto serving tray later.) Cover mold with cookie sheet; turn upside down, then gently lift off mold. Chill until serving time.
4 Slide mold from cookie sheet onto serving tray, lifting and pushing mold at the same time with a spatula moistened with water. Fill center of ring with a small dish of mayonnaise or salad dressing; garnish with salad greens, if you wish.

Tips for the hostess: Make this mold a day or even two ahead, as it will hold well in the refrigerator.

Buttercup Biscuits

A quick shaping trick turns refrigerated biscuits into these three-bite dainties

Bake at 450° for 10 minutes.
Makes 26 tiny rolls

2 packages refrigerated plain or buttermilk biscuits
3 tablespoons butter or margarine, melted

1 Separate the 10 biscuits from each package; cut each biscuit into quarters; shape each quarter into a small ball.
2 Place each 3 balls into ungreased tiny muffin-pan cups. (You'll have 2 balls left; bake for a cook's nibble.) Brush rolls with melted butter or margarine.
3 Bake in very hot oven (450°) 10 minutes, or until golden. Remove from cups. Serve hot.
Tips for the hostess: Rolls may be made ahead and heated just before serving this way: Place in a paper bag; sprinkle bag *very lightly* with water; fold bag over to close tightly. Heat in moderate oven (350°) 10 minutes.

June Rose Wedding Cake

This beauty can be yours with just a little time and some practice. The results are well worth the effort.

Makes 100 servings

Special Items You Will Need
1 three-tier cake pan set
   (7x2¼; 10x2¾; 13x2½ inches)*
2 loaf pans, 9x5x3 inches each
1 five-cup mold
   (6 inches wide, 3 inches deep)
1 cake-decorating set, with:
   Pastry bag; coupling; 6 tubes*
1 plastic turntable, about 15 inches*
3 rounds of heavy cardboard: 14, 10, 7 inches
* These items available in most large department and hardware stores.

(continued)

Preparation Plan
Your cake may be made in three days, following our easy-does-it plan, leaving plenty of time for you for other wedding activities. If you wish to bake, decorate, and freeze the cake two or three weeks before the wedding, be sure to measure your freezer space first. The cake is 14 inches wide and 15 inches tall.

1st day—Bake GROOM'S CAKE; cool; wrap.
2nd day—Bake POUND-CAKE LAYERS
      —Brush all cakes with APRICOT GLAZE
      —Cut and wrap take-home pieces of
        GROOM'S CAKE
      —Make BRIDAL ROSES
3rd day—Assemble cake

Handy Notes for Baking Cakes
Different sets of cake pans will vary in volume. In the set we used, measuring to the brim, the 13-inch pan holds 24 cups, the 10-inch holds 14 cups, and the 7-inch holds 7 cups. Measure your pans with water to determine the volume of each. Each package of pound-cake mix makes about 3½ cups of batter.
Each pan should be filled half full with batter.

Making the Decorations for the Cake
If this is to be your first experience with a cake decorating set, it would be wise to prepare half the recipe for DECORATOR'S FROSTING and practice the various designs before you start your cake. A little practice and you suddenly become a pro and save that sunny disposition.

Bridal Roses
Prepare DECORATOR'S FROSTING *(recipe follows)*. Using half the amount, divide frosting between 2 small bowls. With a few drops of red food coloring, tint one bowl a pale pink and the second bowl a deeper pink. Following the directions that follow, make 36 ROSEBUDS and 30 FULL-BLOWN ROSES.
Allow roses to dry on paper squares on cooky sheet for 2 hours, or until they are firm enough to peel off paper and place on cake.

Groom's Cake

The top tier of our wedding cake is made of fruit cake batter. This is the cake that traditionally is saved for the first anniversary. Our recipe makes this cake and two loaf cakes. The loaves are each cut into 25 thin slices and each slice cut in half. These pieces may be packed in wedding cake boxes or wrapped in trans-

A **June Rose Wedding Cake** with roses cascading from the top tier is a lovely way to start off a marriage.

parent wrap, then silver paper and tied with silver cord as mementos for the guests.

Bake at 275° from 2 hours,
15 minutes to 2 hours, 45 minutes.
Makes one 6x3-inch cake
and two 9x5x3-inch loaves

2 jars (1 pound each) mixed candied fruits
1 package (15 ounces) golden raisins
2 cans (3½ ounces each) flaked coconut
2 cups chopped walnuts
2 packages pound cake mix
4 eggs
1 cup liquid
2 tablespoons apricot brandy
    BRANDY-APRICOT GLAZE (recipe follows)

1 Grease generously and flour a round 5-cup mold, 6x3 inches. Grease and line 2 loaf pans, 9x5x3 inches, with wax paper; grease paper.
2 Combine mixed fruits, raisins, coconut, and chopped nuts in a very large bowl or kettle. Add 1½ cups dry pound cake mix and toss to coat fruits and nuts evenly with mix.
3 Prepare pound cake mix with eggs, liquid called for on label, and apricot brandy, following label directions.
4 Pour batter over prepared fruits and nuts and stir gently until evenly mixed.
5 Divide batter among prepared mold and loaf pans. Place one oven rack in center of oven and arrange all three pans on same rack of oven.
6 Bake in very slow oven (275°) for 2 hours, then begin to test cakes. The cakes are done when a cake tester or long wooden skewer is inserted into center of cake and comes out clean. (The cake may be done in another 15 minutes or may take up to 45 minutes longer.

The time varies with the brand of cake mix you use and the size and shape of your oven.)
7 Remove layers from oven and cool on wire racks for 30 minutes. Loosen cakes around edges with a thin-blade sharp knife and turn out onto racks; remove wax paper; cool cakes completely. Brush with BRANDY APRICOT GLAZE.
Note: If not assembling cake at once, you may wrap cooled cakes in foil or transparent wrap; refrigerate or freeze. The cake will stay fresh and moist for one month in the refrigerator and up to three months in the freezer.

(continued p.88)

1. For Rosebuds: *For each rose, use a small amount of frosting to secure a two-inch square of wax paper to the top of a small jar. Fill pastry bag with pink frosting. Fit #61 tube into pastry bag. Hold tube so larger end touches center of paper. Gently press frosting out of tube while turning the jar to form the tight center of the bud.*

2. *Press out 3 small petals, overlapping around center. Continue to shape 3 to 6 more petals to form a tight, unopened bud.*

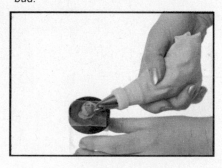

3. For Full-blown Rose: *Fit the #124 tube onto pastry bag. Hold the tube with the wider end touching the center of the paper. Gently press frosting out of the tube, as in Step 1. Center formed with this tube will be slightly open.*

4. *Press out 3 petals around the slightly open center. They should partially overlap one another around the center. Then tilt top of tube (the narrow end) outward as you continue to work.*

5. *Following the same procedure used for the first 3 petals, continue pressing out petals. Shape each additional petal slightly larger than the last. As you continue, you will create the effect of a rose as it would naturally unfold.*

6. *To finish the full-blown rose, press several more petals around those already formed. Tilt the pastry tube so that these petals slant in a more outward position than any of the others.*

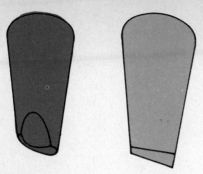

How to Make the Decorative Edgings

You will find your decorating will be more professional if you work out the designs on the frosting with a wooden pick. Then it is simple to follow the design with the pastry bag.

Drop Flowers—Fit the #96 drop flower tube or #27 star tube onto pastry bag. Holding the tube about 1/16 inch away from cake, squeeze, relax pressure, pull tube away. Continue all around tier (*see* FIG. 3).

Fluted Scallops—Fit the #27 star tube onto pastry bag. Following marked-out pattern, press out frosting all around tier.

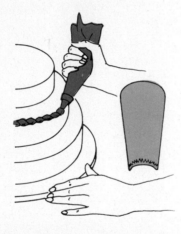

Shell Border—Fit the #98 shell tube onto pastry bag. Press out frosting in overlapping shell design around entire top edge of tier (*see* FIG. 1).

Leaves—Fit the #67 leaf tube onto pastry bag. Press out frosting with a backward and forward motion, then break off pressure with a quick motion to make pointed tip of leaf (*see* FIG. 4).

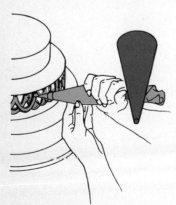

String Scallops—Fit the #2 writing tube onto pastry bag. Mark out scallop pattern in a double scallop. Press out frosting, following design, making single scallop all the way around. Follow with second scallop row to make double scalloping (*see* FIG. 2).

Diamond Pattern—Using same #2 writing tube, follow marked-out pattern, pressing all lines in one direction first, then following with crisscross lines to complete pattern.

Pound-Cake Layer

Bake at 325° from 1 hour
to 1 hour and 30 minutes.
Makes 3 tiers—7-, 10-,
and 13-inches each

6 *packages pound-cake mix*
12 *eggs*
Liquid as label directs
3 *tablespoons apricot brandy*
BRANDY APRICOT GLAZE (recipe follows)

1 Grease and line tiered cake pans with wax paper; grease paper and then dust with flour, tapping out excess. (An extra step, but very helpful to ensure smooth sides on larger cake layers.)
2 Prepare 2 packages pound cake mix with 4 eggs, liquid called for on label, and 1 tablespoon apricot brandy, following label directions.
3 Pour batter into middle tier pan to half fill the pan. If there is additional batter, pour into largest pan.
4 Repeat Step 2 twice. Pour batter into largest pan to half fill the pan, then half fill the smallest pan. (Any extra batter may be baked as cupcakes for a family treat.)
5 Arrange one oven rack in top third of oven and the second rack in the bottom third of the oven. Place largest cake pan on bottom rack in center of oven. Place middle-size pan at back left of top rack and smallest pan at front right of top rack. (Be sure pans do not touch each other, door, sides, or back of oven.)
6 Bake in slow oven (325°) for 1 hour. Then begin to test layers. The cakes are done when a cake tester or long wooden skewer inserted into the center of each cake layer comes out clean. (Baking times will vary with the width and depth of individual cake pans and also the size and shape of your oven.) All layers should be baked by 1 hour and 30 minutes. If the layers on the top rack are getting too brown but do not test done, cover layers lightly with a piece of foil for the last part of baking.
7 Remove layers from oven and cool on wire racks for 20 minutes. Then line wire racks with towels. Loosen each cake around edge with a thin-blade, sharp knife. Turn cake pan on side and shake layer gently to be sure cake has loosened from pan. Turn out layer onto towel-lined wire rack and peel off wax paper. Cool cake completely. (Towel-lined wire racks make it much easier to handle the larger cakes.)
8 Brush tops and sides of layers with BRANDY-APRICOT GLAZE.

Note: If not assembling cake at once, you may wrap cooled layers in foil or transparent wrap and freeze. Unfrosted cake layers may be frozen for up to three months.

BRANDY-APRICOT GLAZE

Makes about 1¼ cups

1 *jar (12 ounces) apricot preserves*
¼ *cup apricot brandy*

Heat apricot preserves until very warm in a small saucepan. Stir in apricot brandy. Strain. The glaze adds flavor to cakes, and helps retain moisture.

WEDDING CAKE FROSTING

Makes enough to frost June Rose Wedding Cake

1 *cup (2 sticks) butter or margarine*
¾ *cup vegetable shortening*
3 *packages (1 pound each) 10X (confectioners' powdered) sugar*
½ *teaspoon salt*
¼ *cup milk*
3 *tablespoons apricot brandy*
3 *tablespoons light corn syrup*
1 *tablespoon vanilla*

1 Beat butter or margarine and shortening until soft in a large bowl. Beat in 10X sugar and salt until mixture is crumbly and all of the sugar has been added.
2 Add milk, brandy, corn syrup, and vanilla. Beat until mixture is smooth and spreadable.

Note: Keep every bowl of frosting *covered* with a dampened paper towel.

DECORATOR'S FROSTING

Makes enough to decorate June Rose Wedding Cake

½ *cup (1 stick) butter or margarine*
½ *cup vegetable shortening*
2 *packages (1 pound each) 10X (confectioners' powdered) sugar*
¼ *teaspoon salt*
3 *tablespoons milk*
2 *tablespoons apricot brandy*
2 *tablespoons light corn syrup*
1 *teaspoon vanilla*

1 Beat butter or margarine and shortening until soft in a large bowl. Beat in 10X sugar and salt until mixture is crumbly and all sugar has been added.
2 Add milk, brandy, corn syrup, and vanilla to bowl. Beat until mixture is very thick and smooth.

To Assemble Wedding Cake

1 Place 14-inch cardboard round on turntable. (Cardboard between each layer makes cutting easier.) Center largest POUND-CAKE LAYER on cardboard. Frost top and side thinly with WEDDING CAKE FROSTING.
2 Center 10-inch cardboard round on cake layer and top with middle cake layer; frost. Center 7-inch cardboard round on cake and top with smallest cake layer; frost. Center 6-inch GROOM'S CAKE on top; frost. This thin basic coat of frosting keeps any stray crumbs in place, and provides a smooth base for final frosting. Allow frosting to dry at least one hour.
3 Frost cake all over with a smooth; thick layer of the WEDDING CAKE FROSTING.
4 Follow designs for cake as we decorated it, or work out your own pattern.
5 Put a small amount of DECORATOR'S FROSTING in each of two small bowls; then tint one a pale pink and the other a pale green with red and green food colorings. Reserve.
6 Fit the #98 shell tube on pastry bag; fill bag with part of remaining frosting (either WEDDING or DECORATOR'S). Pipe a large mound of frosting onto the center of top tier of cake. Peel FULL-BLOWN ROSES off wax paper and arrange, alternating shades of pink, onto frosting mound.
7 Press several small mounds of frosting onto middle cake tier; arrange more roses; Building up from these roses, press out mounds of frosting and place roses on cake side going up from this tier level to meet roses on top. (Should roses start to slide, press a new mound of frosting, arrange roses into frosting and hold in place several minutes until frosting begins to set.)
8 Then arrange roses on bottom tier and build up to meet middle tier of roses. Peel ROSEBUDS off wax paper. Pipe a dot of frosting at intervals, following cake design, on bottom and middle tiers, and press in ROSEBUDS.
9 Fit the #27 star tube onto your pastry bag; fill bag with pink frosting. Press out tiny flowers at intervals, following design.

10 Fit the #67 leaf tube onto pastry bag; fill bag with green frosting. Pipe leaves onto cake, following our picture.
Now your cake is ready to serve. If cake is to be served in a day or two, cover loosely with transparent wrap and keep in as cool a place as possible.
   If cake is to be frozen, place in freezer just as it is, and allow to freeze until frosting is very firm, then cover cake completely with foil, or transparent wrap. Remove cake from freezer the day before the wedding and remove wrappings. When cake has thawed, it can be lightly covered with transparent wrap.

To Cut Your Wedding Cake

1 Start at bottom tier and remove roses. Cut a 3-inch-wide strip all the way around cake. (Bottom and second tier will now be even.)
2 Slice strip into 1-inch-wide pieces; place on serving plate. Cut roses into pieces and add part to each cake slice.
3 Next cut strip from second tier in the same way and slice.
4 Remove the fruit cake tier and save for the first anniversary. Cut pound cake under fruit cake tier into small wedges, then remove cardboard and slice second pound-cake tier into small wedges. Remove cardboard and cut last layer into small pieces.

To Decorate Ceremonial Cake Cutters

Choose a silver or silver-plated cake or pie server or carving knife. Decorate the handle by winding narrow satin ribbon around and round the handle. Insert tiny lilies of the valley and end with bows and a few strands of ribbon.

Party Drinks

Whatever the occasion, giving a party is fun—if you've taken care of all the small details. One of the most important is the beverage. In these pages are alcoholic and non-alcoholic drinks that take away the slightest worry.

NON-ALCOHOLIC FRUIT DRINKS

Cypress Fling

A fizzy drink with a sweet-sour flavor

Makes 8 to 10 servings.

1 can (6 ounces) frozen concentrated orange juice
1 ½ cups water
1 can (12 ounces) apricot nectar
1 bottle (28 ounces) lemon-lime-flavor carbonated beverage

Combine all ingredients in a large pitcher; pour over ice cubes in tall glasses.

Apricot Mist

Floating fruit adds interest to this punch

Makes about 50 punch-cup servings.

1 can (46 ounces) apricot nectar
1 can (46 ounces) pineapple juice
3 cans (6 ounces each) frozen concentrate for limeade
3 bottles (28 ounces each) ginger ale

Combine apricot nectar, pineapple juice, and concentrate for limeade in a punch bowl; stir in ginger ale. Add ice cubes; float a few lime slices and whole strawberries on top, if you wish.

 Party drinks that please: **Claret Cup, Celebration Punch,** and **Cider Cup.**

Cherry Cheerer

Party perfect for children

Makes 4 to 6 servings.

1 envelope cherry-flavor soft-drink crystals
1 26-ounce bottle cola beverage

Combine ingredients in a large pitcher, stirring until all drink crystals are dissolved. Pour over ice in tall glasses.

Cranberry Mist

Just right chilled

Makes 6 servings.

1 can (about 1 pint 2 ounces) pineapple juice
1 16-ounce bottle cranberry juice cocktail
Lemon slices to garnish

Mix pineapple juice and cranberry juice cocktail in a large pitcher, pour over crushed ice in tall glasses and garnish with lemon slices.

Cranberry-Lemon Frost

Scoops of sherbet add creaminess and a pleasing tang to this party refresher

Makes about 18 punch-cup servings

1 bottle (32 ounces) cranberry juice cocktail
2 cans (12 ounces each) apricot nectar
½ cup light corn syrup
1 pint lemon sherbet
Mint sprigs

1 Combine cranberry juice cocktail, apricot nectar, and corn syrup in a large pitcher. Chill at least 3 hours.
2 Just before serving, pour mixture into a punch bowl. Scoop or spoon lemon sherbet into small balls; float on top. Garnish with a cluster of mint.
Tip: If you have a freezer, save yourself last-minute fussing by shaping sherbet balls ahead. Place in a single layer on a cookie sheet; cover with transparent wrap; freeze until serving time.

Cider Cup

Go festive and make a colorful Orange Ice Ring to float in your punch bowl

Makes about 30 punch-cup servings

Orange Ice Ring (directions follow)
8 cups apple cider
1 can (12 ounces) frozen concentrate for imitation orange juice
1 cup light corn syrup
1 bottle (28 ounces) ginger ale
Mint sprigs

1 One or two days ahead, make *Orange Ice Ring* so it will be frozen firm.
2 Combine cider, imitation orange juice, and corn syrup in a large pitcher. Chill at least 3 hours.
3 Just before serving, pour mixture into a punch bowl; stir in ginger ale. Add ice ring. Garnish with a few sprigs of mint.

ORANGE ICE RING
Thinly slice 1 small seedless orange; arrange slices in a circle in a 5-cup ring mold. Pour in ½ cup water; freeze until firm. Add enough cold water to fill mold; freeze. To remove from mold, dip mold *very quickly* in and out of hot water; invert onto a plate.

Wikiwiki Punch

True to its name, it's ready about as fast as you can flip the lids from bottles

Makes 16 large punch-cup servings

3 cans (6 ounces each) frozen concentrate for lemonade, thawed
2 bottles (about 28 ounces each) ginger ale
2 bottles (about 28 ounces each) quinine water
1 cup bottled grenadine syrup
Ice
½ lemon, sliced
½ lime, sliced
Fresh mint

1 Combine concentrate for lemonade, ginger ale, quinine water, and grenadine syrup in a large bowl.
Add a large *Ice Mold* (directions below) or several trays of ice.

This may be a brandy snifter, but **Raspberry Sparkle** is a non-alcoholic drink.

2 Thread each lemon and lime slice with a sprig of mint; float on top. Serve in paper cups.

ICE MOLD
The day before your party, fill a 6- or 8-cup mold with water; freeze until firm. To remove from mold, dip *very quickly* in and out of a pan of hot water; invert onto a plate, then add to punch bowl.

Raspberry Sparkle

Weight-watchers: Sip with a clear conscience, for each glass is just 18 calories

Makes 4 servings

3 envelopes (1½ packages) low-calorie raspberry-flavor gelatin
2 cups hot water
2 cups cold water
3 tablespoons lime juice
Ice cubes
Lime wedges

1 Dissolve gelatin in hot water in a pitcher; stir in cold water and lime juice. Pour over ice cubes in 4 tall glasses.
2 Garnish each with lime wedges threaded onto a kebab stick.

Spiced Peach Punch

Cinnamon and cloves provide a Christmas flavor

Makes 12 servings

1 46-ounce can peach nectar
1 20-ounce can orange juice
½ cup firmly packed brown sugar
3 three-inch pieces stick cinnamon, broken
½ teaspoon whole cloves
2 tablespoons bottled lime juice

1 Combine peach nectar, orange juice, and brown sugar in a large saucepan. Tie cinnamon and cloves in a small cheesecloth bag; drop into saucepan.
2 Heat slowly, stirring constantly, until sugar dissolves; simmer 10 minutes. Stir in lime juice.
3 Ladle into mugs. Garnish each with thin strips of orange rind threaded onto cinnamon sticks, if you wish. Serve warm.

Hot Mulled Cider

Have the serving bowl at the door and hand each guest this hot punch

Makes 16 servings

4 quarts apple cider
1 cup firmly-packed brown sugar
9 whole cloves
9 whole allspice
4 cinnamon sticks, broken into 1-inch pieces
2 lemons, thinly sliced

Tie cloves, allspice and cinnamon in a cheesecloth bag; place in a large kettle with cider and sugar; simmer 5 minutes. Just before serving, remove spice bag. Serve in mugs, and float a lemon slice in each.

PARTY PUNCHES

Claret Cup

Put out your best crystal for this delicious-flavored punch

Makes about 25 punch-cup servings

½ cup Curaçao liqueur
1 can (46 ounces) lemon pink Hawaiian punch, chilled

1 bottle (4/5 quart) claret, chilled
1 bottle (1 pint, 10 ounces) lemon-lime carbonated beverage, chilled
  Ice ring (recipes follow)
1 orange, cut into thin slices

1 Mix Curaçao and punch in bowl.
2 Just before serving, add claret and carbonated beverage; carefully slide in *Ice Ring* and add orange slices.

CLEAR ICE RING
Fill a 6- or 8-cup ring mold with water; set in freezer for 4 hours, or overnight, or until frozen solid. To unmold, let stand at room temperature about 5 minutes, or until ice ring is movable in mold. Invert onto a cookie sheet and slide carefully into filled punch bowl.

STRAWBERRY ICE RING
Pour water to a depth of ¼ inch into a 6- or 8-cup ring mold; freeze about 20 minutes, or until firm. Arrange about 8 whole strawberries on top of frozen layer; pour in ¾ cup water; freeze. To keep berries in place, keep adding water, a little at a time, freezing after each addition, until mold is filled. Freeze until solid. To unmold, let stand at room temperature about 5 minutes, or until ice ring is movable in mold. Invert onto a cookie sheet and slide carefully into filled punch bowl.

Glogg

A Swedish festive drink now an American favorite

Makes 12 punch-cup servings.

1 bottle (4/5 quart) dry red wine
½ cup seedless raisins
  Thin rind from ½ orange
8 whole cloves
1 half-inch piece stick cinnamon
10 cardamom seeds, coarsely broken
1 bottle (4/5 quart) aquavit
10 pieces loaf sugar
  Whole blanched almonds

1 Combine wine and raisins in a large saucepan. Tie orange rind, cloves, cinnamon, and cardamom seeds in a small double-thick cheesecloth bag. Add to saucepan; cover. Heat very slowly just to simmering; simmer 15 minutes. (Do not boil.) Remove spice bag.
2 Heat aquavit slowly in a medium-size saucepan.
3 Place sugar in a large chafing dish. Pour

(continued)

about ½ cup of the hot aquavit over top. Ignite with a match; let stand until sugar dissolves. Stir in hot wine mixture and remaining aquavit.
4 Ladle into heated punch cups, adding a few raisins and one or two almonds to each serving. Serve warm.

Celebration Punch

Save this for a special occasion

Makes about 25 punch-cup servings.

½ cup light corn syrup
½ cup brandy
1 bottle (4/5 quart) sauterne, chilled
1 bottle (28 ounces) carbonated water, chilled
1 bottle (4/5 quart) champagne, chilled
    Ice cubes or Ice ring
2 cups (1 pint) whole strawberries, washed (not hulled)

1 Mix corn syrup and brandy in punch bowl until well-blended; stir in sauterne.
2 Just before serving, add carbonated water and champagne. Carefully add ice cubes or slide in ice ring; add strawberries.

Mulled Wine Punch

Go easy on the brandy—there's plenty of flavor without a heavy hand

Makes about 15 punch-cup servings.

1 bottle (1 quart) cranberry juice cocktail
½ cup granulated sugar
½ cup firmly packed light brown sugar
½ stick cinnamon
6 whole cloves
6 whole allspice
1 bottle (4/5 quart) Burgundy

1 Mix cranberry juice and sugars in a large saucepan. Tie spices in a square of cheesecloth and add to saucepan; heat to boiling, uncovered; reduce heat; simmer 5 minutes. Discard spice bag.
2 Add Burgundy; heat until piping-hot (*do not boil*). Ladle into heatproof pitcher for serving. To keep hot, serve in mugs.

Wassail Bowl

The original Christmas drink

Makes 25 punch-cup servings.

12 small red apples
 3 whole cloves
 3 whole allspice
 3 cardamom seeds, coarsely broken
 1 three-inch piece stick cinnamon, broken
 2 bottles (1 quart each) ale
 1 teaspoon ground ginger
 1 teaspoon ground nutmeg
 2 cups sugar
 1 bottle (4/5 quart) dry sherry
 6 eggs, separated

1 Place apples in a shallow baking pan. Bake in moderate oven (350°) 20 minutes, or until tender but still firm enough to hold their shape. Set aside.
2 Tie cloves, allspice, cardamom seeds, and cinnamon in a small double-thick cheesecloth bag. Place in a kettle with 2 cups of the ale, ginger, and nutmeg. Heat very slowly 10 minutes; remove spice bag. Stir in remaining ale, sugar, and sherry. Heat slowly 20 minutes. (Do not boil.)
3 Beat egg whites until they stand in firm peaks in a large bowl. Beat egg yolks well in a second large bowl; fold in egg whites. Slowly beat in hot ale mixture until smooth.
4 Very carefully pour into a large punch bowl; float baked apples on top. Ladle into heated mugs or punch cups. Serve warm.

Coffee Punch Parisienne

Keep this hidden until after the food is gone

Makes 16 punch-cup servings.

3 cups regular strength coffee
2 cups apple juice
1 cup apricot brandy
¼ teaspoon ground ginger
2 bottles (7 ounces each) ginger ale

1 Combine coffee, apple juice, brandy, and ginger in a large saucepan. Heat slowly just to simmering; remove from heat.
2 Stir in ginger ale. Ladle into heated small mugs or punch cups. Serve warm.

INDEX